Conducting Substance Use Research

POCKET GUIDES TO
SOCIAL WORK RESEARCH METHODS

Series Editor
Tony Tripodi, DSW
Professor Emeritus, Ohio State University

Determining Sample Size
Balancing Power, Precision, and Practicality
Patrick Dattalo

Preparing Research Articles
Bruce A. Thyer

Systematic Reviews and Meta-Analysis
Julia H. Littell, Jacqueline Corcoran, and
Vijayan Pillai

Historical Research
Elizabeth Ann Danto

Confirmatory Factor Analysis
Donna Harrington

Randomized Controlled Trials
Design and Implementation for
Community-Based Psychosocial Interventions
Phyllis Solomon, Mary M. Cavanaugh, and
Jeffrey Draine

Needs Assessment
David Royse, Michele Staton-Tindall, Karen
Badger, and J.Matthew Webster

Multiple Regression with Discrete Dependent
Variables
John G. Orme and Terri Combs-Orme

Developing Cross-Cultural Measurement
Thanh V. Tran

Intervention Research
Developing Social Programs
Mark W. Fraser, Jack M. Richman, Maeda
J. Galinsky, and Steven H. Day

Developing and Validating Rapid Assessment
Instruments
Neil Abell, David W. Springer, and
Akihito Kamata

Clinical Data-Mining
Integrating Practice and Research
Irwin Epstein

Strategies to Approximate Random Sampling
and Assignment
Patrick Dattalo

Analyzing Single System Design Data
William R. Nugent

Survival Analysis
Shenyang Guo

The Dissertation
From Beginning to End
Peter Lyons and Howard J. Doueck

Cross-Cultural Research
Jorge Delva, Paula Allen-Meares, and Sandra
L. Momper

Secondary Data Analysis
Thomas P. Vartanian

Narrative Inquiry
Kathleen Wells

Structural Equation Modeling
Natasha K. Bowen and Shenyang Guo

Finding and Evaluating Evidence
Systematic Reviews and Evidence-Based
Practice
Denise E. Bronson and Tamara S. Davis

Policy Creation and Evaluation
Understanding Welfare Reform in the
United States
Richard Hoefer

Grounded Theory
Julianne S. Oktay

Systematic Synthesis of Qualitative Research
Michael Saini and Aron Shlonsky

Quasi-Experimental Research Designs
Bruce A. Thyer

Conducting Research in Juvenile and Criminal
Justice Settings
Michael G. Vaughn, Carrie Pettus-Davis, and
Jeffrey J. Shook

Qualitative Methods for Practice Research
Jeffrey Longhofer, Jerry Floersch, and
Janet Hoy

Analysis of Multiple Dependent Variables
Patrick Dattalo

Culturally Competent Research
Using Ethnography as a Meta-Framework
Mo Yee Lee and Amy Zaharlick

Using Complexity Theory for Research and
Program Evaluation
Michael Wolf-Branigin

Basic Statistics in Multivariate Analysis
Karen A. Randolph and Laura L. Myers

Research with Diverse Groups:
Diversity and Research-Design and
Measurement Equivalence
Antoinette Y. Farmer and G.
Lawrence Farmer

Conducting Substance Use Research
Audrey L. Begun and Thomas K. Gregoire

AUDREY L. BEGUN
TOM GREGOIRE

Conducting Substance Use Research

OXFORD
UNIVERSITY PRESS

OXFORD
UNIVERSITY PRESS

Oxford University Press is a department of the University of Oxford.
It furthers the University's objective of excellence in research, scholarship,
and education by publishing worldwide.

Oxford   New York
Auckland   Cape Town   Dar es Salaam   Hong Kong   Karachi
Kuala Lumpur   Madrid   Melbourne   Mexico City   Nairobi
New Delhi   Shanghai   Taipei   Toronto

With offices in
Argentina   Austria   Brazil   Chile   Czech Republic   France   Greece
Guatemala   Hungary   Italy   Japan   Poland   Portugal   Singapore
South Korea   Switzerland   Thailand   Turkey   Ukraine   Vietnam

Oxford is a registered trademark of Oxford University Press
in the UK and certain other countries.

Published in the United States of America by
Oxford University Press
198 Madison Avenue, New York, NY 10016

© Oxford University Press 2014

Library of Congress Cataloging-in-Publication Data
Begun, Audrey L.
Conducting substance use research / Audrey L. Begun and
Thomas K. Gregoire.
pages cm.—(Pocket guides to social work research methods)
Includes bibliographical references and index.
ISBN 978-0-19-989231-0 (alk. paper)
1. Substance abuse—Research—Methodology.   I. Gregoire, Thomas K.
II. Title.
HV5809.B44 2014
362.29072—dc23
2013038317

1 3 5 7 9 8 6 4 2
Printed in the United States of America
on acid-free paper

Preface

We knew at the outset that developing a single, unified resource for social work researchers about engaging in the science of substance use and addiction was an ambitious goal. We also wondered if covering the landscape in a single volume was feasible—a "breadth versus depth" debate ensued. We ultimately elected to lean more heavily on the side of "breadth" because of our intended audience: scholars who are moving into this area of study either as new researchers or as researchers experienced in other topical areas. For this reason, we aim to help social work researchers broaden their understanding of how the science of substance use and addiction transpires as they develop their own forms of inquiry in the area of substance use, substance use disorders, and substance-related problems. Therefore, as a scholar's substance-related research becomes more focused, specific issues and skill sets may need to be explored in greater depth. Toward this end, we have identified additional resources and tools that provide greater depth where needed.

Because of our keen interest in and commitment to what has variously been called "moving from theory to practice," "knowledge dissemination and utilization," "bridging the research–practice gap," and "from bench to bedside," we adopted a translational science context for the contents of this book (more about this in chapter 1). With constant awareness of this translational science context, we have organized the book's chapters around key steps in the research process: (1) the background and rationale for developing a study, (2) study design decisions, (3) participant recruitment and retention practices, (4) measurement and analysis decisions, and (5) planning for dissemination, diffusion, and implementation.

We have placed considerable emphasis on what is unique about how social work researchers develop and implement their inquiries about substance use or addiction. This includes, but is not limited to, emphasizing evidence to inform practice, biopsychosocial approaches, life span perspectives, the importance of representative and culturally competent studies, and multilevel integration in social work intervention and inquiry. Each chapter addresses real-world contexts of substance use research and incorporates much of the meaning and experience that we have gained from engaging in substance use research ourselves, learned from the mistakes and accomplishments of peers and colleagues engaged in these endeavors, and received through shared glimpses into the lives of many study participants.

Finally, a note about what this book is not: It is not a review of substance use and addiction research findings, nor is it a book detailing best practices in substance use and addiction prevention or treatment. While we make reference to specific studies addressing these issues throughout the book, we do not pretend to present a systematic, critical analysis of the evidence available to inform practice; there are other, excellent resources available to meet that particular end (e.g., McNeese & DeNitto, 2012; Miller, 2009; Miller, Forcehimes, & Zweben, 2012; Straussner, 2013; van Wormer & Davis, 2013; Vaughn & Perron, 2013). Our aim, instead, is to help inform social investigators about the possibilities for best research practices in the substance use and addiction arena.

Contents

Conducting Substance Use Research

1

Introduction to Conducting Substance Use Research

This book is about conducting social work research involving substance use and substance use disorders, along with substance-related concerns. This topic is particularly relevant to social work investigators because substance-related issues arise in almost every conceivable social work practice domain: Social work practitioners encounter alcohol, tobacco, and other drug-related problems in their work with individuals, couples, families, communities, social institutions, policies, and global systems, whether or not substance use is their primary practice emphasis (Amodeo, Fassler, & Griffin, 2002; Bina et al., 2008; Senreich & Straussner, 2013; Smith, Whitaker, & Weismiller, 2006; Sun, 2001). Social work practitioners and researchers encounter substance use and related issues in their work concerning mental and physical health, child and family welfare, interpersonal and community violence, homelessness, aging, ability and disability, adolescents and emerging adults, employee assistance, criminal justice, and human diversity, among others. According to data collected in the United States' annual National Survey on Drug Use and Health during 2011,

- 8.7% of the population aged 12 years and above (an estimated 22.5 million persons) used an illicit drug during the month prior to responding to the survey—similar to rates in 2009 and 2010
- 2.4% of individuals aged 12 and above (about 6.1 million persons) engaged in the nonmedical use of prescription psychotherapeutic drugs, such as stimulant, sedative/tranquilizing, or pain relief medications
- 22.6% of persons aged 12 years and above (about 58.3 million individuals) participated in binge drinking at least once in the 30 days before responding to the survey
- 8.0% of persons aged 12 years and above (an estimated 20.6 million individuals) met diagnostic criteria for abuse or dependence on alcohol and/or other substances (Substance Abuse and Mental Health Services Administration, 2012b, using *Diagnostic and Statistical Manual of Mental Disorders*, fourth edition, Text Revision, criteria)

Recent and pending changes in the behavioral health care system associated with passage of The Patient Protection and Affordable Care Act of 2010 pose both challenges and opportunities for transforming how treatment for substance use disorders is delivered. Systems of care involving public funding are likely to experience the greatest immediate impact, with mandated inclusion of substance abuse service as an essential benefit that states must offer (Buck, 2011). The number of individuals eligible for publicly funded substance use disorder–treatment services will likely expand greatly as the mandated changes are implemented in 2014 (Buck, 2011); substance use–related services for privately insured individuals may also become increasingly accessible, contributing to increased numbers needing services (Garfield, Lave, & Donohue, 2010). Furthermore, many programs and practitioners providing substance use disorder–treatment services are likely to encounter increased pressure to engage in practices supported by evidence of effectiveness, efficacy, and efficiency to meet mandated criteria and standards of care. In turn, this evolution leads to an enhanced need for social work research to inform, evaluate, and implement innovative interventions.

Alcohol and other drug issues are ubiquitous among the client systems that social work investigators study, regardless of the investigators' primary areas of inquiry. Substance misuse and substance use disorders are often the defining characteristic of the most intractable client problems, and co-occurring problems are commonly presented. The delivery systems for substance use disorder treatment are complex and facing a period of rapid evolutionary transformation. Support for social work investigators' efforts to study substance use–related topics best begins with an examination of the contexts within which such research is conducted and of several issues that investigators are likely to encounter.

SUBSTANCES OF CONCERN

The different types of substances that human beings can abuse are, unfortunately, ever growing and expanding. Known substances of abuse are frequently classified in terms of their mechanisms of effect on the human mind and body. Some of the common categorization schemes include the following:

- tobacco/nicotine (i.e., cigarettes, cigars, pipe tobacco, snuff, and chew)
- alcohol (ethyl), ethanol, or EtOH (e.g., beer, wine, spirits, and caffeinated alcohol mixes)
- cannabis/cannabinoids (i.e., marijuana and synthetically produced compounds)
- opiates/opioids (e.g., morphine, prescription pain medication, and opioid addiction medications such as methadone)
- (psycho)stimulants, amphetamines, and cocaine (e.g., methamphetamines, khat, "crack" cocaine, caffeine, "bath salts," and prescription drugs for attention deficit disorder and narcolepsy such as Adderall, Concerta®, Ritalin)
- hallucinogens and "psychotomimetics" (e.g., lysergic acid diethylamide [LSD], peyote, psilocybin, phencyclidine [PCP], large doses of dextromethorphan cough medicine, and salvia)
- club and synthetic drugs (e.g., gamma-hydroxybutyrate [GHB], ketamine, Rohypnol, 3,4-methylenedioxy-methamphetamine [MDMA] or "ecstasy," amyl/butyl nitrite, Spice, smart/eco drugs, synthetic cannabis/marijuana, and mephedrone)

- depressant and dissociative drugs (e.g., prescription drugs for preanesthesia, sleep, and anxiety/stress such as benzodiazepines, tranquilizers, and sedatives)
- steroids (i.e., anabolic and androgenic steroids)
- inhalants, such as household and industrial aerosol sprays, gasoline, butane (e.g., cigarette lighter refills), nitrous oxide and medical anesthetics (e.g., whipped cream dispensers, "whippets," gas cylinders), and refrigerant gases

Sometimes, listings of commonly abused substances separately categorize prescription medications such as central nervous system (CNS) depressants, stimulants, and pain relievers; sometimes they incorporate misused prescription drugs within the listed categories as defined by the drugs' specific actions. For more details regarding street names, mechanisms of administration, mechanisms of misuse, acute effects, and associated health risks of each type, see the National Institute on Drug Abuse Commonly Abused Drugs Chart at http://www.drugabuse.gov/drug-pages/drugsofabuse.html, their InfoFacts series that provides detailed descriptions of many specific substances of abuse (http://www.drugabuse.gov/publications/term/160/DrugFacts), and textbooks such as Rassool (2011), McNeece and DiNitto (2012), and Miller, Forcehimes, and Zweben (2011). In addition, the National Institute on Alcohol Abuse and Alcoholism Web site provides resources specific to the misuse of alcohol.

As well as understanding the nature of specific substances of abuse, it is often important in substance use research to distinguish between various mechanisms by which substances are being administered. For example, tobacco may be administered by being smoked as cigarettes and cigars or in the form of smokeless tobacco; alcohol may be consumed as wine, beer, "hard" liquor, alcohol–caffeine mixes, or a "jello shot" (see Box 1.1). Substances of abuse may be smoked, ingested, injected, inhaled, absorbed through nasal and oral membranes, as well as across the skin (*transdermal* administration). Distinctions in the routes of administration may be relevant to

- patterns and etiology of misuse and addiction (e.g., intensity of the "high" from injecting or smoking cocaine versus snorting)
- acute and long-term health effects (e.g., acute and long-term brain damage associated with "huffing" solvents or aerosols;

Box 1.1 The Caffeinated Alcoholic Beverage Story

Beverages containing high levels of caffeine entered the United States' drinking scene in 1997 with the introduction of the "energy drink" Red Bull (Thombs et al., 2010). In large numbers, college-aged drinkers engaged in the practice of mixing energy drinks with alcohol: The increased stimulation effects of the caffeine and other additives allowed them to increase their "recreational" alcohol consumption since it took longer for them to experience the subjective alcohol-related effects that would encourage them to stop drinking. This, in turn, increased the potential for high-risk drinking and alcohol-related harm (Berger, Fendrich, Chen, Arria, & Cisler, 2010; O'Brien, McCoy, Rhodes, Wagoner, & Wolfson, 2008). Epidemiologic and etiologic studies quickly led to advocacy for campus- and state-level policy responses to the packaging, labeling, and distribution of beverages with premixed alcohol and "energy drink" components. The full story demonstrates the multiple levels involved: from individual consumption behavior to macro-level responses to these products, including the international influence from other nations like Australia.

immediate cardiac and blood pressure effects versus longer-term dental problems associated with heavy methamphetamine use)
- concomitant risks (e.g., infectious disease exposure from injection of drugs and from sexual contact associated with acquiring or using certain drugs)
- macrosystem factors, including policies, and disparities in treatment service or criminal justice system responses

WHAT SOCIAL WORK BRINGS TO THE ARENA

The National Institutes of Health (NIH) Plan for Social Work Research characterizes social work research as an important and underdeveloped component of inquiry that could positively impact the nation's health (http://obssr.od.nih.gov/pdf/SWR_Report.pdf). The report's authors indicate that social work research "often examines cross-cutting foci" and

Historically, social work research has focused on studies of the individual, family, group, community, policy and/or organizational level, focusing across the lifespan on prevention, intervention, treatment, aftercare

and rehabilitation of acute and chronic conditions, including the effects
of policy on social work practice. (p. 5)

What makes a particular study, line of investigation, or body of knowledge specifically social work, however, remains unclear. The term *social
work research* may refer to the disciplinary identity of scholars conducting
the work. The Action Network of Social Work
Education and Research (ANSWER) additionally describes social work
research in terms of (1) our target audiences, including consumers,
practitioners, policy makers, educators, and the general public; (2) the
societal issues examined, including substance use; (3) exploration of
social, behavioral, and environmental connections and interrelationships
among individuals, families, neighborhoods, and social institutions;
(4) efforts to identify strategies and solutions, as well as informing best
service delivery and public policy practice approaches, to enhance the
well-being of individuals, families, and communities; and (5) the many
types of settings in which our research is conducted (see http://www.
socialworkers.org/advocacy/answer/).
    Social work research also encompasses

- the study of social work practices and the investigation of
  concepts and/or theories that influence social work practices and
  services delivered by social workers
- factors affecting access to services and service coordination
- studies concerning the populations and social systems (at
  multiple levels) with whom and with which social workers
  interact
- research concerning preventive or treatment interventions that
  social workers may deliver
- factors related to the dissemination and utilization of "exemplary"
  social work practices
- methods for improving social work research (e.g., research
  designs, measures, analytic approaches)

Authors of the NIH program announcement for Research on Social
Work Practice and Concepts in Health (see PA-06-081 at http://grants.nih.
gov/grants/guide/pa-files/PA-06-081.html) recognized several important factors that characterize social work research. One important note

relates to the biopsychosocial underpinnings of our profession and how crucial this can be to forging new approaches to intervention, capturing the integration across and interactions between behavioral, psychological, social, social environmental, and physical factors as determinants of wellness and improved outcomes. The announcement's authors also recognized social work as a profession with significant expertise in working across systems of care, within interdisciplinary teams, and with diverse populations who may experience multiple or complex sets of problems. Promoting organizational, community, and social institutional responsiveness to social problems is a significant aspect of the social work profession.

Additional core tenets of the social work profession offer important and relevant contributions to substance use research. The first is that social work practitioners utilize the best evidence available to inform their professional practices (Gambrill, 2004). This includes evidence from multiple sources—client self-determined choices, practitioner wisdom based on practice experience, professional ethics, and research- or empirically based evidence (Gray, Plath, & Webb, 2009; van Wormer & Thyer, 2010). A critical aspect of the research- or empirically based evidence domain lies in the identification of best practices, as well as the conditions and circumstances under which these best practices are likely to work or to fail (Gambrill, 2004; van Wormer & Thyer, 2010). It becomes incumbent on the profession to contribute to both developing and critically analyzing the evidence base concerning best practices with diverse populations, under diverse conditions, within diverse contexts (Gambrill, 2004). This obligation applies also to the social work profession's role in developing functional integration across service delivery systems (Fogel & Roberts-DeGennaro, 2011).

A second key tenet is the life span perspective frequently adopted in social work. Substance use and substance use disorders affect the functioning of individuals at all phases of life: prior to conception and prenatally; during all phases of infant, child, and adolescent development; and during emergent, early, middle, and late adulthood periods. Furthermore, exposure during earlier phases of the life span can have long-term implications for later phases, in both direct and indirect pathways of influence, as we recognize from decades of research concerning the lifelong effects of fetal alcohol exposure (Warren, Hewitt, & Thomas, 2011) and more recent studies of how early life stress contributes to the vulnerability to adolescent problem drinking and substance use disorders in early adult-hood (e.g., Enoch, 2011). The conduct of intervention research concerning substance use is greatly facilitated by certain philosophies, values, and perspectives around which the social work profession is centered. The 2008 Code of Ethics of the National Association of Social Workers lists six core values, the constellation of which reflects the profession's unique purpose and perspective (www.naswdc.org/pubs/code/code.asp, see Preamble). Included among these are social justice, dignity and worth of the person, and importance of human relationships. For example, evidence indicates the importance of certain common therapeutic elements that promote certain common therapeutic factors such as self-determination, self-directed goals, and therapeutic relationship dimensions in determining intervention outcomes (Barth et al., 2012).

An area where social work stands to make still greater contributions in substance use research is to move beyond separate studies of meso- and macrosystem factors toward conducting multilevel and multisystemic studies. This shift allows for a more holistic understanding of substance use, misuse, addiction, and related social or behavioral health problems. Additional dimensions are important for social work investigators to consider as they also have significance for the lives of individuals, families, communities, institutions, and global societies affected by substance use, addiction, production, distribution, related side effects, and treatment. One of these important dimensions relates to policy. The Alcohol Policy Information System sponsored by the National Institute on Alcohol Abuse and Alcoholism (see http://www.alcoholpolicy.niaaa.nih.gov/) summarizes state-by-state and federal policy in 35 policy areas. Social work scholars may need to know, for example, about differences in how health care services for alcohol-related illnesses and treatment of alcohol use disorders are financed in order to understand disparities between states and across population groups. Or researchers may need to know about differences in how taxation or retail sale controls might affect alcohol misuse and related epidemiological patterns. The way in which enacted policies are actually enforced in a community is also an important facet of the picture.

A second important dimension for researchers to consider involves possible disparities across subgroups and populations (e.g., age, gender, race/ethnicity, social class, and life circumstances). These disparities relate to patterns of use, addiction, access, norms, and treatment related to a particular substance. For example, 20 states in the year 2010 had provisions pertaining to child abuse or neglect related to a woman's alcohol use during pregnancy (see http://www.alcoholpolicy.niaaa.nih.gov/ Alcohol_and_Pregnancy_Legal_Significance_for_Child_Abuse_Child_ Neglect.html). Knowing about this stance when conducting research concerning women's substance use may contribute to a better understanding of the impact of disparities in how women access treatment services for substance use disorders or prenatal health care.

Another example where social work researchers encounter significant disparities involves access to addiction treatment services experienced by individuals during incarceration in jail or prison and as incarcerated individuals reenter the community following release from custody. Despite the relatively high rate of substance use and substance use disorders among individuals in jails and prisons, they receive remarkably few evidence-informed services, even though these have demonstrated efficacy and effectiveness for improving quality of life and reducing recidivism (see LeBel, 2010; Re-Entry Policy Council, 2004). Furthermore, there exist marked discrepancies in terms of how jail and prison inmates' race and ethnicity compare to the nation's general population (Minton, 2011). Because of our social justice perspectives, social work researchers may lead the substance use research field to ask questions that are very different from those traditionally pursued.

ADOPTING A TRANSLATIONAL SCIENCE FRAMEWORK

An oft-repeated theme in substance use research involves the need to ensure that what we learn through science is translated into practice improvements. We have adopted a broad-spectrum framework of translational science as applied to substance use science, a framework adapted from several models presented in the scientific literature (e.g., Wandersman et al., 2008). First, the framework that we offer covers a wide range of knowledge-building activities designed to address questions that span the full translational science spectrum and then some. These activities are iterative in nature; they have mutual, back-and-forth influences on one another. All of a researcher's activities and decisions, from which research questions are asked through disseminating outcomes, are affected by "where the science is."

Brekke, Ell, and Palinkas (2007) present a two-phase conceptual model for understanding translational research. The first phase incorporates "lab knowledge to clinical intervention trials" (efficacy, effectiveness, and best practices). The second phase incorporates "adoption of best practices in the community" (dissemination/diffusion and implementation). Below, we present an overview of activity domains that we include as aspects of a translational science cycle organized somewhat differently, but compatibly, with the Brekke et al. (2007) conceptual model. In our representation, it is important to recognize that each phase is related to the others in iterative patterns of influence.

Epidemiology and Exploration

These investigative activities help us "begin at the beginning" by identifying patterns and trends in the appearance or emergence of new problems with substance use, as well as concomitant, consequential, and co-occurring phenomena. Epidemiology helps us to answer questions about the distribution of the problems across and within populations or groups and how the problems might appear differently among different groups. This phase of research also helps us to identify possible disparities between groups in terms of how our responses and resources to the problem of substance misuse are distributed. Furthermore, this phase of the translational science cycle is often exploratory in nature: In many cases, we need good, detailed, descriptive data concerning the people and emerging problems of concern. One thing that we do know about the epidemiology of substance use is that patterns of use, misuse, and addiction are always changing (Alemagno, 2009). Always fluid are statistics concerning who is using what, when, where, and how, as well as what we know about substance use concomitants and consequences.

In the substance use literature, a scholar is likely to run into the word *epidemic* being applied to the problems of substance use and addiction. In the science of substance use, an additional concept, that of "syndemic,"

> Before you build a better mousetrap, it helps to know if there are any mice out there.
>
> –Yogi Berra

has been applied to the complex epidemiological patterns being observed. *Syndemic* refers to the ways in which a set of enmeshed, intertwined social and physical conditions interact synergistically to intensify negative conditions and "disease burden" in a population—far more than would be predicted from a simple biomedical model (Singer, 2009). Singer (2009) argues that the dynamics of social inequity, poverty, and marginalization create syndemic public health conditions. In order to understand population disparities in one condition (for example, acquired immunodeficiency syndrome [AIDS] expression among women who abuse noninjection drugs), other interactive circumstances experienced within that population must also be considered (for example, human immunodeficiency virus [HIV] exposure risks associated with sex-for-drugs exchanges; HIV exposure risks associated with different forms of sexual contact; HIV resistance reduction related to poor nutrition, alcohol use, and other substance-related health challenges; mental health and cognitive impairment problems affecting women's sexual risk assessment and self-protective behavior practices). The problem with many current research approaches is a conventional tendency to focus on one disease at a time, ignoring the salient interacting conditions in studies of etiology and treatment (Singer, 2009).

Etiology

Etiological research activities are concerned with identifying the natural course or trajectory of substance-related disorders. Research in this arena may address, for example, how substance use disorders develop and resolve; identification of vulnerability, risk, resilience, and protective factors specific to substance use disorders; potential mediator and moderator influences on substance use outcomes; and the interactional nature of varied biological, psychological, and social factors. Etiology may also be reflected in the examination of genetic and epigenetic models. Epigenetic processes are those which modify genetic expression (*phenotype*) without affecting the underlying gene sequence (*genotype*). Epigenetic research, often interdisciplinary in nature, provides opportunities for synthesis across the social environmental and biological bases of substance use and addiction. It is important for the field of substance use research in general that multilevel, multisystem, integrative, holistic models of etiology be

> You think because you understand "one" you must also understand "two,"
> because one and one make two. But you must also understand "and."
>
> –Rumi

adequately examined: We do not necessarily understand "the whole" just because we understand a multitude of parts.

Intervention

Intervention research includes multiple phases of study, as well as being relevant across the prevention–treatment continuum. According to the NIH program announcement PA-06-081 mentioned earlier, social work intervention includes psychosocial and combination approaches to screening, assessment, and early intervention; treatment of disorders (including reduced residual symptoms, enhanced symptom management, improved functioning); posttreatment support to maintain treatment gains and behavior changes over time (including relapse prevention and management of comorbid symptoms); and improvement in treatment or rehabilitation services access, quality, and outcomes. In addition, they include for consideration approaches that target behaviors of service/treatment providers, improve quality of care, or enhance service delivery at the supervisory, systems, and organizational levels.

Additional information about specific skills related to intervention research can be found in the book by Fraser, Richman, Galinsky, and Day (2009). Research in the intervention phase can be considered within three domains which help bridge the gap between research and practice (Carroll & Rounsaville, 2003): intervention design, efficacy studies, and effectiveness studies. A stage model of development can be helpful in thinking about the relevant research activities (Rounsaville, Carroll, & Onken, 2001).

- *Intervention Design*. A relatively early phase involves the initial designing, planning, and development of innovative intervention strategies at any possible level of intervention (e.g., intraindividual, families, groups, neighborhoods, institutions, larger communities, policy) or at multiple levels in an integrated fashion. Intervention design, planning, and development generally begin with a theoretical basis for hypotheses about what could work and why it should work. The process generally concludes with relatively small-scale pilot testing of intervention protocols that can be manualized and standardized to some degree. Results of pilot testing are used to further modify and develop the intervention approach in an iterative feedback process. Pilot testing may involve quasi-experimental or full experimental designs, or combinations of these approaches, including multiple single-system studies.

- *Efficacy Studies.* A second phase of intervention research involves studies designed to test the nature and extent of impact of an intervention, as well as to identify side effects or complications associated with the intervention approach. Efficacy studies typically rely on traditional experimental study designs and methodologies that minimize within-group variability; in other words, they work with carefully selected participants and systematically trained interventionists who exhibit a high degree of protocol fidelity. These approaches help us to determine those observed outcomes that can be reasonably attributed to the specific intervention under study.
- *Effectiveness.* A subsequent phase in programs of intervention research involves studies designed to test the extent to which satisfactory outcomes can be achieved under real-world circumstances. Sometimes this is referred to as "taking to scale" an efficacious intervention, but it involves more than numbers of persons served: It also involves expanded population diversity, increasingly typical intervention delivery conditions, and less control exerted over factors such as clients' co-occurring problems and previous treatment histories. A significant question to be addressed in the course of effectiveness studies relates to the degree of fidelity to the intervention protocol that is expressed in real-world practice, as well as the nature of and need for deviation from the intervention's standards.

Implementation and Adoption

The translational science cycle is incomplete without addressing questions regarding the factors which influence the adoption of intervention approaches which have proven to be efficacious and effective. Chapter 5 elaborates on this particular topic. The Network for Improvement of Addiction Treatment is an example of a group targeting barriers to the adoption and implementation of effective approaches that might exist at the practitioner, program, and service delivery system levels (see www. niatx.net). A helpful overview of how implementation science applies to intervention research is provided by Dearing (2009). Arenas in the implementation and adoption category relate to studies of the following:

- *Dissemination and Diffusion.* This body of research examines best practices for making practitioners, communities, policy makers, and others aware of and prepared to utilize innovative approaches to address substance use problems. A lot may have changed with the advent of so many social networking tools, and there are significant implications in the research for how we prepare practitioners both to engage in specific evidence-informed practices and to pursue evidence-informed practice in general.
- *Implementation and Adoption.* These studies examine factors involved in the application of evidence-informed or evidence-based interventions by practitioners, communities, policy makers, and others. Research has proven over and over again that the principle "if you build it, they will come" does not apply to the adoption and implementation of evidence-informed practices for intervening with substance use–related problems.
- *Deadoption.* This process is concerned with practitioners, programs, communities, and policies where an innovation has been discontinued after a sincere trial or even a prior period of adoption. While it is helpful to know how to change poor practices, it is important to know when, why, and how we lose good ones, too.
- *Cost.* An important subset of intervention-adoption questions to consider involves the cost-effectiveness, cost-benefit, and efficiency dimensions associated with particular intervention approaches.

Research for and about Research

Finally, our ability to engage in any research activities, including all aspects of the translational science cycle, is dependent on new developments in

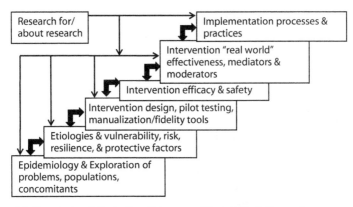

Figure 1.1 Translational Cycle for a Program of Social Work Research.

research technology. This includes innovations in research design, participant recruitment and retention, study design and methodology, measurement, data analysis, and other research practices. We have chosen to categorize these knowledge-building activities as research "for and about" research (see Figure 1.1).

THE COMPLEXITY OF SUBSTANCE USE PROBLEMS

Clearly, the design and methodology of any particular substance use study are dependent on "where the science is" in that particular area of knowledge building. Integrated across our translational science framework is another important knowledge-building dimension: what we know about the entire molecular-to-global continuum of substance use and addiction factors. One of the factors affecting all of practice and research in substance use is the nature of co-occurring phenomena: the interplay with other critical circumstances, such as crime and violence at the community and interpersonal levels, child welfare concerns, comorbid mental health conditions, and public or physical health risks and complications. The complexity of problems related to substance use also tends to require addressing multi-, inter-, and transdisciplinary approaches in both interventions and research. Substance use research is often improved through the engagement of the practice community and other constituents in the research-development process.

The complexity of substance use and addiction is reflected in the complexity of federal research funding responses. Substance use–related programs of research are supported by numerous actors in the community of government grantors across many "basic" and "applied" science arenas. These include, but are not limited to, the National Science Foundation and various agencies under the Department of Health and Human Services (DHHS). Within the DHHS, among the 2012 funding leaders were several that have at various times included substance-related research in their portfolios: the NIH, the Centers for Disease Control and Prevention, the Substance Abuse and Mental Health Services Administration, the Administration for Children and Families, and the Health Resources and Services Administration. The remaining DHHS agencies that funded research during 2012 also may have interests in substance-related research: the Agency for Healthcare Research and Quality, Food and Drug Administration, Administration on Aging, Indian Health Service, and Center for Medicare & Medicaid Services.

Zeroing in on the NIH, the complexity picture becomes even more evident. In the past, among the 21 institutes (plus six centers), many had funding portfolios that included aspects of substance use research. Most notable have been the National Institute on Alcohol Abuse and Alcoholism, the National Institute on Drug Abuse, and the National Institute on Mental Health. However, related research has also been funded through the National Cancer Institute, the National Human Genome Research Institute, the National Institute on Aging, the Eunice Kennedy Shriver National Institute of Child Health and Human Development, the National Institute on Minority Health and Health Disparities, and possibly other disease- or profession-specific institutes. Outside of the DHHS is situated the National Institute of Justice, under the Department of Justice's Office of Justice Programs. The National Institute of Justice also has a history of funding substance use research initiatives across the translational science continuum.

Three predominant and cross-cutting themes spanning all of these substance-related research funders are emphases on (1) translational science; (2) inter-, multi-, and transdisciplinary science; and (3) co-occurring phenomena (e.g., comorbid disorders, mental and physical health concerns, intimate partner violence, community crime and violence, health disparities, and child development/welfare concerns).

Social work researchers are advised to become informed about another important aspect of substance use about which practitioners, policy makers, and law enforcement professionals are often reminded: the fluid, dynamic, variable nature of substance use trends and patterns over time (both historical and cohort effects), across subgroups and populations, and by regional geography. The nature, names, and access to various drugs fluctuate dramatically as well.

For example, according to the National Survey on Drug Use and Health (Substance Abuse and Mental Health Services Administration, 2010), the prevalence estimate for lifetime use of inhalants reported by those 18–25 years old differed significantly in just the 7 years between 2002 (15.7%) and 2009 (10.7%). Or, for example, the observation that binge drinking was reported by 14.8% of adults in the United States during 2003 masks the fact that these drinking patterns are far more commonly encountered in some geographical areas than others: according to the Centers for Disease Control and Prevention, the 21.8% rate in Wisconsin is far greater than Tennessee's 8.2% rate (http://www.statemaster.com/graph/ hea_alc_con_bin_dri-health-alcohol-consumption-binge-drinkers). Additionally, patterns of use and rates of disorders often differ within substate geographical regions: urban, suburban, rural, and those with versus without college campus populations.

Variability in the phenomena under study has significance to all phases and aspects of the research enterprise: analytic reviews of existing literature, research questions asked, selection of study design elements (particularly sampling and measurement decisions), and conclusions regarding generalizability of results. For these reasons, and others, it is critical for social work investigators to engage the local practice community and other representative constituents in planning, as well as implementing, substance use–related research studies.

GREAT DEBATES IN THE SUBSTANCE USE ARENA

Anyone venturing into the substance use research arena needs to become reasonably informed about the major debates or schisms that they likely will encounter. Some of these have long, complex histories and others are quite recent developments. Several are introduced below; more in-depth critical analysis of these debates is a worthwhile pursuit for scholars planning to engage in substance use–related research.

Addictive Substances versus Addictive Behaviors

This great debate is connected to the question, What are the meaningful distinctions between behaviors that are *habits, compulsive behaviors,* and *addictions?* There is little controversy these days as to the addictive nature of many substances; alcohol and other drug addictions are no longer considered "bad habits" by most researchers and interventionists. However, there exists some reluctance to include other "behavioral addictions" in the same category as substance use disorders: behaviors such as problematic gambling, sex, eating, Internet use, and other "compulsive" behaviors that share some overlapping biological and psychological features with substance use disorders (Grant & Portenza, 2005).

Harm Reduction

The debate regarding harm reduction essentially has two significant components in the United States. The first is a policy-level concern, whereas the second is expressed at the level of providing treatment to individuals. In essence, the concern is whether or not it is preferable to develop and implement policies that address the social problems associated with substance use rather than sinking tremendous resources into stopping substance misuse at its root, acknowledging that we have not been successful in eliminating substance misuse in our society. Some examples of this sort of policy practice include

- needle exchange programs that may reduce infectious disease transmission without direct impact on rates of injection drug use
- offering free substance analysis to reduce the rate of overdoses and bad drug reaction deaths without stopping the use of the tested substances
- providing free taxi service and better late-night public transportation to intoxicated bar patrons to reduce impaired driving incidents without affecting the rate of drinking to excess
- providing access to homeless shelters to individuals regardless of their willingness to commit to modifying their drinking and drug use

At the individual treatment level, the approach acknowledges that complete abstinence is not a goal for some individuals, at least initially. Intervention objectives relate to making changes that will reduce the quantity and/or frequency of their substance use without necessitating complete abstinence or eliminating the consequences associated with their substance misuse, such as by eliminating the use of substances in risky situations (e.g., while working with dangerous equipment or while responsible for the well-being of children or other dependents) or by substituting a less risky prescription medication for the risky "street" drug being abused (see "Preventing Harm" in Miller et al., 2011). One concern is that these approaches may represent "slippery slope" practices that circumvent the true objective: stopping substance misuse in our communities and helping individuals achieve and maintain complete sobriety. Some scholars argue that harm reduction is not sufficient: The goal should be harm elimination (Heather, 2006). A recent resource related to harm reduction in substance use and other risk-related behaviors is an edited book, presented in three parts: the history of harm reduction, approaches related to specific substances or service delivery sectors, and international examples (Pates & Riley, 2012).

Abstinence versus Controlled Use as Goals

Closely allied with the harm reduction debate is another great debate concerning the most appropriate treatment and recovery goals in alcohol and other drug treatment interventions: Is "use reduction" a reasonable form of harm reduction, and is "controlled" use possible (see Heather, 2006)? On the one hand, there is considerable anecdotal and etiologic evidence to suggest that individuals who have ever experienced addiction to substances, despite their recovery status, cannot safely expect to be able to engage in controlled use of psychoactive substances at any point in the future—including caffeinated and tobacco products. From this perspective, therefore, the goal of treatment intervention should always be total abstinence and zero tolerance for substance use.

Others are able to present anecdotal and etiologic evidence suggesting that some individuals can achieve controlled use, maintaining sobriety without total abstinence, and that this may be a more realistic goal for some individuals to make as their recovery commitment (see Heather, 2006; Marlatt & Witkiewitz, 2002). As always, the devil lies in the details: the level of confidence in our ability to discern who can and who cannot achieve controlled use is quite inconsistent, the way that "controlled" use is defined, and the time frame over which controlled use is measured (i.e., they will revert back to their substance use disorder; it just has not happened yet). There are also likely to be differences of opinion (and evidence) depending on the substances involved: Most controlled use literature concerns drinking alcohol, not other drugs.

Medical Model and Other Theories

Whichever theories or underlying models are adopted in order to explain a phenomenon like substance use disorders, the theory determines pathways and strategies for prevention and intervention. Historically, a "disease" model of addiction was originally offered to counter a prevailing premise that addiction is a reflection of moral or character flaws in the afflicted individual, and the disease model lies at the heart of the Alcoholics Anonymous movement (Doweiko, 2009; McNeece & DiNitto, 2012). When addiction is viewed as a "disease," one premise invoked is that the problematic behavior is caused by biological pathologies and that the disease continues to exist even if the individual is not presently using the substance of addiction (Doweiko, 2009; McNeece & Di Nitto, 2012). However, detractors argue that no single, specific "disease" process has been definitively identified as the basis for addiction and that so many subforms of the "disease" exist that any attempts to classify addiction as a single disease are rendered useless.

In a medical model, on the other hand, the concept of addictive disorders is applied instead of the disease concept. This frees us from the necessity of identifying a single pathogen or cause of the disease and allows us to look at the problem in more complex ways. Medical model interventions typically involve modifying significant brain–behavior relationships, including efforts to modify neurochemistry, motivation, memory, and emotional states. Currently, many argue that addiction disorders fall into the class of chronic, recurring disorders (much like diabetes, for example) and that these disorders may involve multiple problem–recovery–relapse cycles (McKay & Hiller-Sturmhöfel, 2011). Thus, long-term management becomes the goal rather than "cure." Medical model detractors point to personal choice and individual responsibility aspects of substance misuse, an approach that might indicate criminal justice sanctions

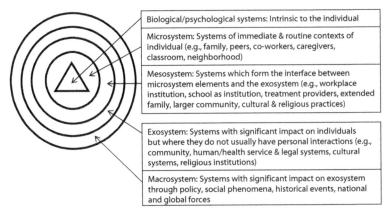

Note: Figure derived from Bronfenbrenner (1979) and Garbarino (1992)

Figure 1.2   Diagram Depicting Interactive Ecological Systems. Figure derived from Bronfenbrenner (1979) and Garbarino and Abramowitz (1992).

as a more salient set of responses than the treatment approaches indicated by a strictly medical model interpretation.

Many other models and theories of substance use disorders have been presented (and variously supported or contradicted) in the empirical literature. One dimension along which the various models differ is in terms of where in an ecological systems perspective their focus is directed (see Figure 1.2). These levels include (1) system elements internal to individuals (i.e., their biological, physiological, neurological, genetic, and psychological systems), (2) interfaces and interactions between individuals and their most immediate and intimate environmental contexts (i.e., immediate family or other central life structures), and (3) how these nuclear system elements are influenced by and interact with successively less intimate systems, institutions, and ecological contexts.

A number of textbooks contain explanations or explorations of historical and contemporary models concerning the etiology of addiction (e.g., McNeece & DiNitto, 2012; Miller et al., 2011; Straussner, 2013; van Wormer & Davis, 2013). Miller et al. (2011) present an integrative public health perspective as one which takes into account aspects of the specific agents (or substances), "hosts" (or individuals), and environmental contexts. This perspective forms the basis for a public health response to

Table 1.1 Categories of Theories and Models of Etiology in Addiction

Model Type	Model Category	Brief Description/Applications
Biological	Agent	Hazardous nature of the substances themselves is the cause of addiction
	Genetic	Vulnerability (propensity) and resilience to addiction are conveyed through genotype; may or may not be substance-specific models involved; can be useful in risk assessment and developing physiological therapies
	Neurobiology	Specific neurochemical pathways (brain and behavior) and/or anatomical areas of the brain are involved in addictive processes; brain–behavior link can be modified therapeutically; comorbidity
Psychological	Moral	A deficit in moral values, strength of will, character flaws; poor lifestyle choices
	Psychodynamic and attachment	Ego deficits, attachment relationship problems, orality as common themes underlying addiction
	Personality	Specific personality traits or dispositions differentiate persons with or at risk of addiction from others; "addictive" personality construct; co-occurring disorders
	Learning	Seeking to repeat direct positive experiences associated with use, avoid negative experiences from withdrawal, despite negative aspects of use (root of cognitive-behavioral model); paired associations between substances and previously neutral stimuli (triggers for relapse)
	Social learning	Learning through observation/modeling, as well as direct experience of rewards and punishments from social environment; learned expectancies; role of media models in music, advertising, fashion, movies, TV, gaming environments, sports
	Cognitive	Cognitive appraisal determines response to stimulus; expectancies affect appraisals; behavior can be changed if appraisals are altered; information processing is affected by substances, which affects behavior; cognitive impairments from substance use affect intervention response

(continued)

Table 1.1 (Continued)

Model Type	Model Category	Brief Description/Applications
Sociocultural	Ethnicity, culture	Social influence; culturally transmitted customs, traditions, values, beliefs; addiction subcultures; social norms; "sub" cultures and deviance norms
	Social networks	Risk and protective factors present as social influences through social networks (family, peers, social institutions); role of supportive significant others in recovery; sobriety networks through treatment groups
	Macrosystem	Structural risk and protective factors within the social context/environment; access to substances; systems of oppression and exploitation; lack of satisfactory alternatives; extreme stressors; service system disparities; economics of drug use at individual, local, regional, national, international levels; access/barriers to intervention programs/services; health disparities issues

problems of substance misuse and addiction. Table 1.1 classifies some of the major addiction etiology perspectives into a biopsychosocial framework to assist new substance use scholars in exploring the literature further.

CHAPTER CONCLUSIONS

Substance-related problems are encountered in all domains of social work practice, in all arenas where social workers are engaged, and often represent a significant barrier to the implementation of effective interventions. Therefore, it is likely that many social work researchers, regardless of their primary areas of study, will wish to investigate research questions that either are centered on or overlap with substance use concerns. In order to perform this type of research well, investigators need to develop knowledge and skills pertinent to research in this arena. Social work investigations are relevant at all points in the translational science process and at all levels of investigation or intervention: the individual, dyad, family, group, neighborhood, organization or institution, policy, and global society. It is hoped that new and emerging social work scholars also will find the topics in substance use research exciting and will choose to direct their own careers in this challenging but tremendously rewarding direction.

2

"Big Picture" Aspects of Design and Analysis in Substance Use Research

Introductory research and grant-writing textbooks generally allot considerable attention to the importance of research designs being closely and logically related to the nature of the research questions being addressed. This remains an equally important issue in the development of substance use research. As outlined in chapter 1, the translational research cycle is characterized by various approaches and types of research questions: epidemiological, etiological, intervention, diffusion, and research-about-research. Chapter 2 is comprised of three major subdivisions. The first presents an overall orientation to the substance use knowledge base and introduces several major studies that appear in the literature. The second section offers ideas for related research designs and explores substance use research design issues. The chapter's third section examines a number of variables that social work investigators might consider when designing substance use studies.

PART I: BECOMING FAMILIAR WITH THE KNOWLEDGE BASE

The first topic concerns how one might approach the task of becoming familiar with existing literature and studies that can inform social work research about substance use. Many of us have our favorite systems for searching literature on a particular topic. Some of the sources by which literature concerning substance use and addiction might be searched include PsycInfo, PubMed, Criminal Justice Abstracts, ERIC, Social Sciences Abstracts (H.W. Wilson), SocINDEX, and Social Work Abstracts, as well as sites that permit simultaneous searches of multiple databases (e.g., Web of Science/ISI, JSTOR, EBSCO, WorldCat, and Google Scholar).

> "Anyone inclined to check wet paint has the right stuff for doing science."
> –Corey S. Powell
> (Editor-in-Chief, *Discover*)

There are many sources of current literature on substance use. A number of journals have the dissemination of substance use–related content as their primary aim. Other journals frequently publish articles with substance use–related content that overlaps with their primary aims, making it necessary to cast a wide net when searching for relevant literature. A listing of journals that often publish articles with substance use–related content, particularly those likely to be of interest to social work researchers, appears in Appendix A.

In addition, a considerable number of public access resources, reviews, and reports are produced either by or for various institutes of the National Institutes of Health, the Substance Abuse and Mental Health Services Administration (SAMHSA), and the Centers for Disease Control and Prevention. An investigator may wish to search the publications resources of the National Institute on Drug Abuse (NIDA) at http://drugpubs.drugabuse.gov/ as well as those provided through the National Institute on Alcohol Abuse and Alcoholism (NIAAA) at http://www.niaaa.nih.gov/publications. Also, SAMHSA offers an array of publications that may assist in developing research studies, particularly intervention studies (see, e.g., http://store.samhsa.gov/home). In 2004 SAMHSA produced a systematic review entitled *Clinical Preventive Services in Substance Abuse and Mental Health Update: From Science to Services.*

While the SAMHSA site can be searched by type of condition, substance type, intervention approach, or research concern, it also may be useful to search their inventory of Treatment Improvement Protocols (TIPS) and Technical Assistance Publications (TAPS). Furthermore, each region of the nation is served by one of 14 regional (and one national) centers in the Addiction Technology Transfer Center Network. The Addiction Technology Transfer Centers (ATTCs) are charged with providing professionals with access to evidence concerning different aspects of addiction prevention and treatment (see www.attcnetwork.org/index.asp).

Another published resource that may provide researchers with initial introductions to specific substance-related topics is the *Encyclopedia of Substance Abuse Prevention, Treatment, and Recovery* (Fisher & Roget, 2009; Miller & Carroll, 2006). The NIAAA's fortieth anniversary edition of *Alcohol Research & Health*, Celebrating 40 Years of Alcohol Research (2010), also provides scholars new to this area with an orienting framework. Representing a decade of research conducted through the National Drug Abuse Treatment Clinical Trials Network (CTN) is a special issue of the *Journal of Substance Abuse Treatment* (see http://www.journalofsubstance-abusetreatment.com for the June 2010 issue, volume 38, supplement 1).

Resources that social work investigators may wish to consult for systematic reviews concerning substance-related intervention studies include both The Campbell Collaboration Library (see http://www.campbellcollaboration.org/) and the Cochrane Collaboration (see http://www.cochrane.org/). Abraha and Cusi (2012) present scholars with a handbook of Cochrane Collaboration reports concerning alcohol and drug misuse.

> "If I have seen a little further it is by standing on the shoulders of giants."
> —Isaac Newton

An example of this type of review is presented in the Cochrane Collaboration meta-analytic review of motivational interviewing and substance abuse (Smedslund et al., 2011). Similarly, a meta-analysis of motivational interviewing appears in the *Research on Social Work Practice* journal (Lundahl, Kunze, Brownell, Tollefson, & Burke, 2010). These reports are relevant because motivational interviewing has developed into an approach that is strongly endorsed by many scholars who study behavioral intervention with individuals experiencing substance-related problems. There are also reviews of 12-step programs (Ferri, Amato, & Davoli, 2006), social norms interventions for college students (Moreira, Smith, & Foxcroft, 2009), and case management for persons with substance use disorders (Hesse, Vanderplasschen, Rapp, Broekaert, & Fridell, 2007). Still other review examples reflect specific populations rather than specific intervention approaches, like the review of psychosocial interventions for pregnant women in alcohol treatment (Lui, Terplan, & Smith, 2008) and the review of intervention with incarcerated individuals (Mitchell, Wilson, & MacKenzie, 2006). Norcross, Krebs, and Prochaska (2011) also provide results of their meta-analytic review of relationships between psychotherapy outcomes and the stages-of-change component of the transtheoretical model of behavior change, which may be of interest to some social work scholars.

OVERVIEW OF MAJOR SUBSTANCE USE STUDIES

There are in the substance use literature several major, large-scale studies with which an investigator might wish to become familiar to develop awareness of both study outcomes and methodological perspectives. The large national and multiyear epidemiological studies are wonderful sources for statistics regarding incidence and prevalence rates in various populations.

A design feature that several of these major studies share is their multisite nature: Developing multisite studies is one creative solution to problems associated with limits on sample size and diversity that may arise with study designs requiring large numbers of participants who meet specific demographic or assessment criteria and where there is not a sufficient population from which to draw. Multisite studies also help address research questions related to effectiveness under real-world conditions, especially where study sites vary in specified, measurable ways. Social work researchers interested in conducting substance use studies may be most effective when their work is conducted through collaborative partnerships between research universities and community-based partners (see Begun, Berger, Otto-Salaj, & Rose, 2010) as well as between collaborators from different regions of the nation.

Arranged alphabetically by study name, here are several large-scale study sources of information and possibly secondary analysis databases to consider.

Bureau of Justice Statistics

Data collected by the US Department of Justice through the Office of Justice Programs and the Bureau of Justice Statistics may be of interest to scholars seeking data regarding substance use patterns and the criminal justice system (see http://bjs.ojp.usdoj.gov/content/dcf/contents.cfm). Their reports provide information concerning drug use patterns, associations between drug use and crime, drug treatment for individuals under correctional supervision, and substance-related variables as measured through different aspects of the criminal justice system (e.g., arrests, jail or prison, postrelease). Unlike some of the national surveys which are aimed at answering specific research questions, the Bureau of Justice Statistics synthesizes data routinely collected by a number of statistical reporting agencies into unified reports.

Collaborative Studies on Genetics of Alcoholism (COGA)

This large-scale, multisite, multipronged series of studies funded by the NIAAA advanced the science of genetic contributions to the risk for alcohol use disorders. Study investigators have collected clinical and biological data from hundreds of families and thousands of individuals. The Collaborative Studies on Genetics of Alcoholism data are available to future investigators to conduct their own analyses. Several chromosomal regions have been identified by the team as containing some number of genes that contribute to both the clinical characteristics of alcohol use disorders and protective factors, as well as those overlapping with co-occurring mental health issues. This large family of studies involved social work researchers in their development and implementation and contributed a new assessment tool called the "Semi-Structured Assessment of the Genetics of Alcoholism" (see http://pubs.niaaa.nih.gov/publications/arh26-3/214-218.htm.

COMBINE Project and COMBINE Cost–Effectiveness

Eleven study sites participated in an NIAAA-funded study of the relative effectiveness of different combinations of two medications (acamprosate and naltrexone) and two behavioral intervention approaches (Anton et al., 2006). The behavioral interventions included either low-intensity medication-management counseling sessions or moderate-intensity, manual-guided combined behavioral intervention, designed as a form of outpatient psychotherapy integrating a variety of evidence-supported methods. Close to 1,400 volunteers experiencing alcohol use disorders and recently abstinent were randomly assigned to one of nine difference treatment or placebo conditions. The study found the greatest degree of support for the use of naltrexone in combination with either medical management or combined behavioral intervention (Anton, O'Malley, Ciraula, Cisler, Couper, Donovan, et al., 2006). Subsequent to the COMBINE Project outcome study, the team also conducted cost–effectiveness analyses concerning the various approaches utilized (Zarkin et al., 2008).

Community Youth Development Study

The Community Youth Development Study was a 5-year intervention study seeking to determine the effectiveness of the Communities That Care intervention in reducing youth drug use, violence, delinquency, pregnancy, and school dropout. The study was funded primarily by NIDA with cofunding from the National Institute of Mental Health, the National Cancer Institute, the Eunice Kennedy Shriver National Institute of Child Health and Human Development, and the Center for Substance Abuse Prevention. The study randomly assigned 24 communities in seven states to either intervention or control conditions. Data collection consisted of annual surveys with 4,407 youth who entered the study in the 5th grade and were followed for 5 years. The study found that risk for negative behavior increased more gradually from 5th to 10th grade for the intervention group and, by the 10th grade, youth in the intervention communities demonstrated significantly lower incidence of alcohol use, delinquent behavior, and tobacco use than youth in the control communities (Hawkins et al., 2012).

Drug Abuse Treatment Outcome Studies (DATOS)

These multisite studies were supported by the NIDA. A number of drug abuse treatment outcome study results that have been reported (see http://www.datos.org/contents.html) address aspects of treatment outcomes related to various client population and treatment characteristics. The Drug Abuse Treatment Outcome Studies collected data from over 10,000 treatment admissions to 96 different facilities. The treatment approaches studied include a wide range of types (e.g., inpatient, outpatient, medication, and drug-free) and populations (e.g., adolescents, adults, women, incarcerated individuals). Study findings included support for the efficacy of substance abuse treatment and for the benefit of a longer stay in treatment (Simpson, Joe, & Brown, 1997). In addition to outcome results, these studies have contributed to our understanding of "during treatment" processes (e.g., time spent in treatment) and how treatment programs function under real-world conditions.

Drug Abuse Warning Network (DAWN)

Conducted by SAMHSA's Center for Behavioral Health Statistics and Quality, the Drug Abuse Warning Network has monitored hospitals' emergency department visits and deaths reported to be drug-related, at least through 2012. One major contribution to practice and research was to serve as an "early warning" system concerning new drugs appearing on the scene, new patterns of substance use, previously unrecognized hazards associated with more familiar substances, and drug combination hazards. Data collected through the Drug Abuse Warning Network included estimates of emergency department visits for drug-related suicide, mortality, and under-age use by substance type. In addition to national-level data analyses, the Drug Abuse Warning Network sampled eight different cities. Data were collected through the Substance Abuse & Mental Health Data Archive (see http://www.samhsa.gov/data/DAWN.aspx), where much of the data are available for direct download.

Monitoring the Future

Funding from the NIDA has supported this annual survey of the nation's 8th-, 10th-, and 12th-grade students. Trends in substance use patterns among adolescents can be examined since 1975, the first year of study (see http://www.drugabuse.gov/related-topics/trends-statistics/monitoring-future). The 2011 survey collected data from over 46,000 students in 400 secondary schools. The surveys ask about usage patterns for a number of substances but also measure attitudes (e.g., perceived risks, approval or disapproval) and perceptions of access to/availability of different substances. These data are a good source of current trends in alcohol and other drug use and patterns of use among American youth. Recently, data about college students and adults (through age 50) have also become available.

National Drug Abuse Treatment Clinical Trials Network (CTN)

The Clinical Trials Network does not consist of a single study but instead represents a network through which multiple studies have been conducted. The NIDA has funded this group of research–practice collaborative partnerships for conducting treatment clinical trials (see http://www.drugabuse.gov/about-nida/organization/cctn/ctn). This site is a good source of current clinical research findings and provides an opportunity for accessing secondary data from prior trials. The network's goal is to provide an infrastructure to encourage multisite studies that can achieve sampling design goals more quickly and facilitate greater diversity among participants than might be feasible in single-site studies. Community treatment programs provide the treatment services being investigated and do so under conditions more representative of "real-world" conditions than might exist in some clinical trial settings. A related goal is to more efficiently move efficacious and effective interventions into adoption by practitioners. The types of intervention approaches that are supported by the network include pharmacotherapies, behavioral interventions, and approaches that combine these types of strategies.

National Drug Abuse Treatment System Survey

Also known as the "Outpatient Drug Abuse Treatment Studies (ODATS)," the National Drug Abuse Treatment System Survey was an NIDA-funded longitudinal study of the programming approaches and organizational structure of a stratified random sample of 413 outpatient drug treatment program conducted in five waves from 1998 through 2005. Data representing waves two through four are publically available (http://www.icpsr.umich.edu/icpsrweb/SAMHDA/studies/4146). The study goals were to determine if current treatment approaches were consistent with best practices and to explicate the organizational factors that influenced treatment practices. Findings have described the organizational characteristics associated with meeting the specific programming needs of racial and ethnic minority groups and women, provision of comprehensive health services, interagency collaboration, and the availability and role of support services such as case management in connecting clients to treatment (Friedmann, Durkin, Lemon, & D'Aunno, 2003; Friedmann, Lemon, Stein, & D'Aunno, 2003b; Lamar & Reed, 1997; Wells, Lemak, & D'Aunno, 2005).

National Epidemiologic Survey on Alcohol and Related Conditions (NESARC)

This large-scale survey funded by the NIAAA was conducted in two waves, 2001–2002 and 2004–2005 (http://pubs.niaaa.nih.gov/publications/AA70/AA70.htm). It addressed alcohol use disorders and "their associated disabilities" across the general population of adults aged 18 years and above. This study consisted of a very large sample size, in excess of 43,000 persons nationally, that allowed for accurate estimates of even infrequent conditions associated with alcohol use disorders. In addition to questions about alcohol, alcohol treatment, and family history of alcoholism, respondents addressed other substances (tobacco and other drugs) and other mental health concerns (major depression, phobias, anxiety and personality disorders, pathological gambling, medical conditions, and victimization). The study contributed to the epidemiology of alcohol use disorders and co-occurring problems, as well as providing data about disparities between groups in the distribution of the problems and service utilization (see *Alcohol Research & Health*, spring 2002 entire issue).

National Survey on Drug Use and Health (NSDUH)

Sponsored by the SAMHSA, this US survey has been conducted since the late 1980s. The reports provide national- and state-level data concerning a range of substances of abuse (tobacco, alcohol, illicit drugs, and prescription drugs), as well as other mental health concerns. In addition, the National Survey on Drug Use and Health oversamples in a select group of states to allow for accurate substate estimates in these areas. Trends for specific substances and/or populations (e.g., by age, ethnicity, gender) can be tracked across time through these reports (see https://nsduhweb.rti.org/RespWeb/project_description.html).

Project MATCH

Funded by the NIAAA, this multisite effort compared three distinct approaches to the treatment of alcohol use disorders: cognitive behavioral, motivational enhancement, and 12-step facilitation (Project MATCH Research Group, 1998). Participants included 952 persons enrolled in outpatient treatment at one of five locations and an additional 774 individuals participating in aftercare treatment following either residential or intensive day treatment. In essence, no systematic significant differences were observed in outcomes related to these three approaches, nor were there many differences based on matching client characteristics to type of treatment approach. Important gains were made with this project, including evidence that treatment works (all three approaches were accompanied by positive results); experience in developing the infrastructure and systems to support large-scale, multisite, multidisciplinary alcohol treatment studies; and treatment manuals supporting each of the different approaches (see http://www. commed.uchc.edu/match).

PART II: DESIGNING SUBSTANCE USE RESEARCH

Conducting Meta-Analyses or Systematic Reviews in Substance Use

Meta-analyses and systematic reviews are two important methods for making important contributions to the substance use literature. Meta-analytic methods provide an opportunity to mathematically combine data from multiple studies, thereby overcoming some of the limitations introduced when small sample sizes result in studies with low statistical power. This approach can result in greater confidence concerning the estimates generated by each study considered alone and provide clarity when there are questions about between-study heterogeneity (Trikalinos, Salanti, Zintzara, & Ionnidis, 2008). In cases where the existing literature does not support the application of solid meta-analytic methodology or the research questions are a little too broad for meta-analysis to be applied, scholars may choose to engage in a methodologically derived systematic review of evidence, applying a clearly identified methodology for identifying, assessing, synthesizing, and interpreting the evidence.

If your scholarship goals involve conducting a systematic review or meta-analysis related to substance use, two recent contributions to the Oxford *Pocket Guides to Social Work Research Methods* series offer important methodological insight. First is the guide *Systematic Reviews and Meta-Analysis* (Littell, Corocoran, & Pillai, 2008) and second is *Finding and Evaluating Evidence: Systematic Reviews and Evidence-Based Practice* (Bronson & Davis, 2011). Another pair of resources to consult are the article by Wells and Littell (2009) and an introductory guide to systematic reviews that includes statistical meta-analysis and meta-ethnography (Gough, Oliver, & Thomas, 2012). These methodologies are quite specific and distinct from the process of becoming familiar with literature in a topic area.

Qualitative and Mixed-Methods Research Strategies

The type of research design that an investigator adopts ideally is determined by the nature of the research questions to be addressed. In topic areas where the knowledge base is minimal and exploratory knowledge-building questions are more appropriate than are experimental questions, qualitative methodologies are most likely the preferred tools to apply. These are the methods that help us understand the people experiencing substance-related circumstances, the nature of their past and present experiences, the cultural base for their interpretation of these experiences, as well as their future expectations and aspirations.

Qualitative research methodologies are also critical starting points for developing the instruments that we might choose to apply in subsequent studies of a more quantitative nature. Furthermore, qualitative methodologies play an explanatory role when systematically used to strengthen, ground, and inform interpretation of findings from studies that also employ quantitative designs. Resources for qualitative and mixed-method approaches to substance use research include the *Journal of Mixed Methods Research* and the journal *Qualitative Research*; others include the book edited by Tashakkori and Teddlie (2003), the book by Padgett (2008), and the review article by Carlson, Siegal, & Falck (1995). Narrative inquiry as a research methodology has great potential utility in social work investigations concerning substance use. An example constructed in this vein is presented by Wilson, Cunningham-Burley, Bancroft, Backett-Milburn, & Masters (2007).

Intervention Research

To a large extent, both the social work profession and the substance use field have embraced the movement to promote greater use of evidence to inform practice. Steenrod (2009) offers an interesting review of how this has played out in the substance treatment arena. Much substance treatment research has focused on answering the question *Does it work?* about specific intervention techniques for reducing or preventing the occurrence of substance use disorders or for promoting recovery from substance use disorders. Two Oxford *Pocket Guides to Social Work Research Methods* may prove useful to the social work investigator interested in asking these kinds of intervention research questions: *Intervention Research: Developing Social Programs* (Fraser et al., 2009) and *Randomized Controlled Trials: Design and Implementation for Community-Based Psychosocial Interventions* (Solomon, Cavanaugh, & Draine, 2009). Other types of substance treatment research questions include the following: *How does it work? For whom does it work?* and *Is it worth the cost?* These types of intervention research questions often call for very different research designs.

> "You've got to be very careful if you don't know where you are going, because you might not get there."
>
> —Yogi Berra

The rigor of a research design is often evaluated on the basis of the design's ability to address concerns with internal validity. In this context, the randomized control trial (RCT) might be seen as the gold standard, within a hierarchy that includes a variety of quasi-experimental and experimental designs along the way (see, e.g., Shadish, Cook, & Campbell, 2002). A complementary criterion for evaluating research designs addresses external validity concerns. Selecting the "best" study design becomes a bit of a balancing act as many of the design options differ in terms of where the validity "controls" are presented. On the one hand, we have studies which restrict many sources of variability as a means of promoting *internal validity*: the extent to which the outcomes can be attributed to the predictor variable or intervention under study, rather than to other confounding, intervening, uncontrolled variables. On the other hand, carefully controlled experimental designs may stray quite a distance from the realities under which interventions are delivered, thereby calling into question a study's *external validity*: the extent to which study conclusions can be generalized to real-world populations and circumstances. Table 2.1 identifies a range of study design options tailored to the type of research question and validity concerns being addressed through each study design.

Related to these study designs is the case of a blinded intervention study. The (single) *blinded* study is intended to reduce the influence of participants' own expectations on the study results: Their expectations of whether or not an intervention will work may bias the results that they report. The *double-blind* intervention study involves procedures to prevent experimenter bias from creeping into outcome results as well. While this is not so difficult to achieve in addiction medication studies, double-blind circumstances can be very difficult to achieve in behavioral intervention research.

One strategy that is strongly encouraged is to ensure that the individuals responsible for collecting data are different from those who deliver the behavioral intervention. Among the concerns addressed, this approach reduces the potential for social desirability bias, which may appear when a respondent becomes motivated to either please the investigator or avoid sanction for reporting negative outcomes. Additional protections ensue when the data collectors remain naive as to which condition each participant experiences; this is improved by separating the data collection and intervention roles.

Despite the design benefits of employing random assignment, it is not uncommon to encounter staff resistance to its use when conducting intervention studies in collaboration with community-based providers. An argument commonly encountered is that it would be unethical to provide the new treatment to one group while providing something different to another group (i.e., those assigned to receive an existing "treatment as usual" or "no treatment control" condition or individuals on a waiting list for services). Implied in this sort of objection is a belief that the new intervention will be effective. However, such claims in the absence of empirical evidence can be of questionable value, and it may be at least as unethical to subject a vulnerable population to an untested intervention. It is important to explore carefully the ethical issues surrounding the use of random assignment. Shadish et al. (2002) provide a thoughtful discussion of the

Table 2.1 Sample Study Design Options in Substance Use Research

Type of Design	Research Goal	Diagram	What Is Addressed
Cross-sectional survey; observation or qualitative study	Describing a group, population, process, or situation at a single point in time	O	Description only
Client satisfaction (survey or interview)	Assessing client opinions of experiences with one intervention	X O	Description only
Case report, case study	Descriptive report of one intervention and outcomes for one or a few cases	$X\ O_{a1...an}$	Description only
Natural "experiment"	Assessing outcomes of a naturally occurring event	[X] O	Description only
Single group posttest only	Assessing one intervention's outcomes with a group of cases	X O	Description only
Single group pretest/posttest design	Longitudinally comparing outcomes with preintervention condition for one intervention	$O_1 X O_2$	Did measured "outcome" states exist prior to intervention
Single-subject or single-system intervention design (ABA design)	Longitudinal series of n preintervention observations (A phase) compared to series of m observations during intervention (B phase) and series of p postintervention observations (return to A condition)	$O_{a1} O_{a2} O_{a3} \ldots O_{an} X_{b1} X_{b2} X_{b3} \ldots X_{bm} O_{a(n+1)} O_{a(n+2)} O_{a(n+3)} \ldots O_{a(n+p)}$	Experimental manipulation of intervention for "n of one" or a small number of cases (practice evaluation)
Comparison group pre-/postintervention design	Cross-sectional comparison of outcomes for one intervention and nonintervention control groups with longitudinal pre- and postintervention observations	$\dfrac{O_1 X O_2}{O_1\ O_2}$	Experimental manipulation of intervention condition; contrast outcomes with preexisting status
Comparison delayed intervention pre-/postintervention group design	Cross-sectional comparison of outcomes for the intervention where untreated comparison group becomes a delayed intervention group	$\dfrac{O_1 X O_2}{O_1 - X O_2}$	Experimental manipulation of intervention condition; contrast outcomes with preexisting status; cohort comparison; durability of outcomes

Design	Description	Notation	Common elements
Randomized controlled trial (RCT)	Cross-sectional comparison of outcomes for randomly assigned intervention and nonintervention control groups, plus longitudinally comparing pre- and postintervention observations	$\dfrac{R\ O_1\ X\ O_2}{R\ O_1\ O_2}$	Preexisting group difference confounds; experimental manipulation of intervention condition; contrast outcomes with preexisting status
Solomon four-group design: RCT, one intervention and two measurement conditions	Cross-sectional comparison of outcomes for randomly assigned intervention and nonintervention control groups plus longitudinally comparing pre- and postintervention observations, plus control for possible repeated measurement influence	$\dfrac{R\ O_1\ X\ O_2}{\dfrac{R\ O_1\ O_2}{\dfrac{R\ X\ O_1}{R\ O_1}}}$	Preexisting group difference confounds; experimental manipulation of intervention condition; contrast outcomes with preexisting status; repeated measurement effect
RCT of different interventions (comparative effectiveness)	Cross-sectional comparison of outcomes for two different randomly assigned treatment conditions with random assignment to group and with pre-/postintervention observations	$\dfrac{R\ O_1\ X_1\ O_2}{R\ O_1\ X_2\ O_2}$	Preexisting group difference confounds; experimental comparison of two interventions; contrast outcomes with preexisting status
RCT of different interventions with postintervention follow-up (comparative effectiveness)	Cross-sectional comparison of outcomes for two different randomly assigned (R) treatment conditions with random assignment to these groups and with pre-/postintervention observations for both groups	$\dfrac{R\ O_1\ X_1\ O_2\ O_3}{R\ O_1\ X_2\ O_2\ O_3}$	Preexisting group difference confounds; experimental comparison of two interventions; contrast outcomes with preexisting status; durability of effects

Cost–effectiveness study: determining the relative cost (in multiple dimensions) of each unit of outcome benefit observed

Meta-analysis/common elements assessment systematic integration of results from multiple studies to determine overall outcomes or advantages associated with specific intervention approaches

Note. O = observation point; X = intervention exposure; R = random assignment to condition; numeric subscript = intervention condition or ordinal sequence of observations.

ethics of random assignment. Other analyses address the significance of "equipoise" in clinical research, when the ethical balance depends on circumstances where we remain equally unsure about the relative benefits of two conditions to which participants might be exposed.

Additional Study Design Options

In addition to seeking maximum control over internal validity threats, other practical and cost–benefit balance concerns come into play with substance use study design. These include such issues as the feasibility of treatment assignment, access to sufficient numbers of participants to fill all of the "cells" in a study design, fidelity to intervention protocols, and costs of implementing different designs. Related to the issue of practicality is the option of developing multisite studies as one solution to generalizability concerns, such as avoiding cross-contamination between participants in different conditions of the study design and providing access to sufficient numbers or diversity of participants. Social work investigators might consider engaging collaborators through some of the following resource networks. The Society for Social Work Research (SSWR) has "Substance Misuse and Addictive Behaviors" as one of its research clusters. The Society for Social Work Research also has a special interest group (SIG) of scholars specifically interested in the topic addictive behaviors and substance abuse, which meets every year at the annual conference and hosts a listserve. The Council on Social Work Education (CSWE) has an addiction-related contents track that hosts a list serve of scholars and educators interested in addictions. The interdisciplinary Research Society on Alcoholism (RSoA) and Association for Medical Education and Research in Substance Abuse (AMERSA) each have a self-identified, semiformal group of social work scholar members with a listserve as well. Furthermore, a number of university-based social work research centers have experience with and research goals involving the conduct of substance-related research, many that might welcome opportunities to engage in collaborative partnerships.

Group Randomization

An important variation on the theme of RCTs bears explaining here: the *group-randomized trial* (Murray, 1998). Group-randomized trials are a class of nested, hierarchical, multilevel, or clustered designs. Like the

RCT, individuals provide the data points. And, like the RCT, which intervention is received by each group is randomly determined. However, the units of randomization are not the individuals but instead the groups to which individuals belong. In other words, the groups themselves are not randomly constructed—there are preexisting connections among members of the groups. For instance, the individuals in a group may be already receiving substance-related treatment services at each of several specific programs or agencies, or they may attend specific schools or live in a community that was randomly assigned to a prevention intervention condition. Another term used to describe these types of studies is the *cluster-randomized study* (Murray, 1998).

This group-level randomization approach may be more practical than individual randomization approaches, especially when there is a strong likelihood of cross-contamination between participants who might have been assigned to different conditions. For example, if the purpose of a study is to test the impact of training intake workers in motivational interviewing approaches to screening, assessment, and feedback, it is quite likely that those trained in the experimental approach will "contaminate" the performance of those in an untrained "control" condition if they work together at the same program or in the same agency. It may therefore be preferable to randomly assign programs to each condition, with all social workers in each program receiving the same condition. Similarly, in intervention studies where it is not feasible to randomly assign across all individuals in a study, it may be possible to randomly assign conditions to specific clusters or types of participants. For example, all clients in a particular addiction treatment program may be assigned to one condition and all clients in another, similar treatment program may be assigned to the other condition, thus creating a cluster-randomized design (Miller, Strang, & Miller, 2010). Another common use of this approach is in prevention studies where schools or even whole communities may be randomly assigned to treatment or comparison conditions. It is important, however, to fully understand the implications of these sorts of nested designs on data analytic strategies (see Murray, 1998). Employing statistical approaches that assume simple random sampling will result in inaccurate findings.

More about Cross-Sectional Designs

One important design consideration in substance use research involves determining when it is preferable to utilize cross-sectional, longitudinal, or integrated data collection design strategies. In *cross-sectional designs*, data are collected at a single point in time. This approach is common in substance use epidemiology studies as well as in certain experimental and quasi-experimental approaches to intervention research. In substance use intervention research, cross-sectional designs are often used to compare different treatment groups at a common point in time, such as between-group comparisons of outcomes for individuals who did versus did not receive a particular intervention. This describes a classic RCT where only outcome data are collected.

In cross-sectional substance use research, the investigator needs to consider what makes a particular data collection point superior to other possibilities. For example, if the research questions are developmental in nature, one might choose the data collection point based on participants' chronological ages (which is simply a measure of time since birth). This approach is adopted in the Monitoring the Future epidemiology series with measurement with three groups of adolescents: one each in the 8th, 10th, and 12th grades. The greatest design-based sources of internal validity threat in cross-sectional studies derive from the many ways in which the groups being compared might have differed from the outset, prior to an intervention.

The cross-sectional approach is subject to at least one major external validity threat as well. In a single round of observations, it is nearly impossible to distinguish between cohort and developmental effects. In other words, are observed age-group differences indicative of developmental phenomena or of cohort differences between the groups? In this context, *cohort* might reflect differences between individuals raised before versus after drinking age legislation changes, cohorts with versus without exposure to universal drug use prevention programs in public schools, or cohorts in emergent adulthood before versus after the significant media coverage of prescription misuse–related deaths of public icons. A cohort is a group whose members share common factors, histories, contexts, and/or experiences that may differ from those of other cohort groups.

It is important for social work investigators to apply "nested" design and analysis approaches if there is a likelihood that participants are subject to any sort of cohort or grouping phenomena. Essentially, respondents in either situation no longer represent independent elements in the design. As a result there is now variability at multiple levels that must be accounted for in the design and analysis. In substance use research, carefully consider the likelihood of various meso- and macrosystem influences on individual group members, such as county or state differences in funding for services; neighborhood differences in access to or advertising of the studied substances; classroom or school-wide "climate" factors; or parenting, family values, and family process factors (see, e.g., Begg & Parides, 2003).

More about Longitudinal Designs

On the other hand, *longitudinal designs* (or panel data) call for repeated measurements conducted with the same participants at two or more time points, such as the same individuals being measured at intake to drug court, at completion of the intervention, and at a 6-month follow-up. Longitudinal approaches address change over time more directly than do cross-sectional studies and can help test the durability of changes if subsequent follow-up data are collected. Implementing longitudinal study designs can be prohibitively expensive, at least in terms of effort exerted to maintain participant involvement over time, and can be relatively impractical if the time frames of the change processes are extensive (e.g., change occurs over decades rather than in months). More about participant retention in longitudinal studies is addressed in chapter 3; suffice it to say here that minimizing validity risks related to participant (and investigator) attrition over time is a paramount longitudinal research issue.

In longitudinal intervention designs each of the individual study participants provides data at multiple time points. In essence, each person serves as his or her own comparison "control" condition, a period when the intervention was not applied. This addresses some of the worrisome internal validity threats introduced through cross-sectional designs. However, the cohort issue raises its ugly head once again: We have no way of knowing if the results are generalizable to other cohorts or are somehow unique to the one cohort studied over time.

In longitudinal, repeated measurement designs we have an additional complication that affects our data analytic strategies. Many quantitative inferential statistical approaches require conformity to an assumption of independence among the observations being analyzed. In the case of repeated measurements we no longer have complete independence among the observations—two or more are being collected from the same individuals. (We still need to have a lack of dependence between individual participants within a time point however.) Longitudinal study designs require analyses adapted to these circumstances; fortunately, we currently have statistical strategies that can be applied when the source of nonindependence is from repeated measures.

In some cases, analysis might be accomplished through the use of repeated measures statistical approaches, such as the paired t test or a repeated measures analysis of variance. If the samples are sufficiently large and distributed appropriately, more contemporary approaches that correct for the longitudinal dependence may be preferable: robust standard errors, generalized estimating equations, random-effects (mixed) models, or fixed-effects models (see, e.g., Allison, 2005). This might be accomplished by treating the variable "time" as one of the grouping levels in testing our models. Some of these latter approaches are more forgiving than the analysis of variance approaches and may help reduce the risk of Type II errors, where we fail to reject the null hypothesis when we probably should have done so. These approaches also may vary in terms of how they handle missing data or unbalanced designs where the number of participants in each panel might not be the same or proportional. They also vary in terms of how they can handle time-variant predictor variables: variables that might change between observation points, like employment, housing, or marital status demographics, or in quantity and frequency of drug use. Some approaches can only manage time-invariant predictor variables, such as the age at which alcohol (or another drug) was first consumed, gender, or ethnic background.

If the outcome of interest in a longitudinal study is whether or not an event occurs, such as when individuals' first initial use of alcohol occurs or the time elapsed between substance treatment initiation and a first relapse episode, the social work investigator may require logistic regression or longitudinal event occurrence or survival analysis strategies. For more details on these approaches to longitudinal methodology, see Guo (2010), Singer and Willett (2003), and Allison (1995).

Typically, single-subject or single-system intervention studies extend the repeated measures longitudinal design: Multiple baseline observations are followed by multiple observation points during the intervention delivery period and then followed up with multiple observation points for a period after termination of the intervention. For more details on this methodology, see Nugent (2010).

Another important consideration in designing longitudinal studies about substance use is related to the "unit of analysis" problem. If a study is answering questions about how an intervention affects individuals, the units of analysis and of data collection are the same: the individuals who are (or are not) exposed to the intervention. For example, we may be interested in analyzing how long individuals remain abstinent from drinking alcohol under three different treatment conditions. However, the unit of analysis might be at the level of neighborhoods, communities, programs, or agencies, even counties, states, or larger geographical regions. In these larger-system studies, "longitudinal" designs might not involve data collection from the very same individuals over time but might instead use a consistent sampling strategy for drawing groups of respondents who represent the particular units of analysis in the design (e.g., different individuals within the same schools, neighborhoods, counties, or states).

Integrative Designs

Clearly, both cross-sectional and longitudinal studies have their associated advantages and disadvantages. For these reasons a more complex (and more expensive to implement) *cross-lag panel design* might be employed, combining both cross-sectional and longitudinal design elements (see Table 2.2). The "panel" component indicates that the same individuals are observed at multiple points in time (see Rubin & Babbie, 2005), whereas the cross-lagged component reflects multiple panels at each observation period.

In this approach, longitudinal analysis of a single intervention (X) is executed through comparison of observations at two time points (O_{a1} with O_{a2}), a simple pre-/postintervention design. This simple design is buttressed, however, through replications with at least two additional intervention cohorts (i.e., comparing O_{b1} with O_{b2} and O_{c1} with O_{c2}). Furthermore, with this complex study design we are also able to answer questions about whether or not the three cohorts started out similarly by comparing their preintervention data (O_{a1}, O_{b1}, O_{c1}, and O_{d1}) as well as whether or not there exist cohort effects in the outcomes: comparing outcomes for the different cohorts (O_{a2}, O_{b2}, and O_{c2}). We can estimate the influence of any repeated measurement effects by comparing the groups that experienced the second-round data collection procedures without also experiencing an intervention (O_{d1} compared with O_{d2}). We are also

Table 2.2 The Cross-Lag Panel Design for Intervention Research

Study Cohort	Observation Period		Observation Period		Observation Period		Observation Period	Observation Period
Cohort $_a$	O_{a1}	X	O_{a2}		O_{a3}		O_{a4}	O_{a5}
Cohort $_b$			O_{b1}	X	O_{b2}		O_{b3}	O_{a4}
Cohort $_c$					O_{c1}	X	O_{c2}	O_{a3}
Cohort $_d$							O_{d1}	O_{d2}

Note. O = observation or measurement point; X = intervention; a–d = which cohort in the design is observed; 1–5 = which number observation in the cohort's series the observation represents.

able to examine the durability of effects associated with the intervention (X) by comparing data from the various follow-up periods (i.e., O_{a2} with O_{a3}, O_{a4}, and O_{a5}; O_{b2} with O_{b3} and O_{b4}; and O_{c2} with O_{c3}).

Intervention Fidelity

In research addressing intervention efficacy, effectiveness, or adoption/ implementation, questions concerning intervention fidelity or verification of the intervention's integrity will undoubtedly arise. The degree to which what actually takes place during an intervention adheres to intentionally designed elements of the specific intervention under study is what is meant by intervention fidelity or the integrity of its delivery. Dobson and Cook (1980) refer to poor intervention fidelity as contributing to Type III error in intervention research studies—inability to determine if inconsistent or absent intervention impact results from poor implementation or inadequacies in the intervention itself. Social work intervention research has been criticized in the past for insufficiently attending to issues of fidelity and treatment integrity (Naleppa & Cagle, 2010). Borrelli (2011) offers researchers important guidance on the issues of assessing and improving fidelity to intervention protocols. Important aspects of intervention fidelity or integrity include

- adherence to the prescribed delivery of program elements
- the amount of exposure to program content that each participant experiences
- the qualities of both the processes and content that are delivered (how well they fit the ideal protocol developed)
- participants' engagement with program components

- features of the intervention as delivered that are uniquely distinguishable or differentiated from other program features (Dane & Schneider, 1998)

To the extent that fidelity can be quantified it becomes a variable to measure, and monitoring of fidelity over time may need to be included in the overall research design. What we do know about fidelity is that it is more easily achieved with intervention protocols that are low in complexity, when interventionists are well trained to the protocol, and when the intervention is perceived as being highly salient and effective by the individual delivering the intervention (Ruiz-Primo, 2006). An example of how fidelity might be addressed in substance use intervention research is the work by motivational interviewing scholars to determine how well an exchange between an interventionist and participant represents the intent of motivational interviews (e.g., Madson & Campbell, 2006; Moyers, Martin, Manuel, Hendrickson, & Miller, 2005; Wallace & Turner, 2009). In studies where training of staff takes place, addressing the fidelity to training protocols also is of great importance (Baer et al., 2007).

Mechanisms of Change Research

In many instances, knowledge-building efforts of intervention research are ready to move beyond demonstrations of efficacy and effectiveness and toward research that allows us to examine specific mechanisms of change: moving from what works and how much it works to questions about how and why interventions work or fail and for whom do they work best or least. Ultimately, investigations of change processes can help us to develop intervention strategies that are better informed about the essential elements or critical ingredients common to our evidence-informed practices. This becomes essentially a question of opening the "black box" of intervention: We deliver an intervention (input) and we see the results or outcomes (output), and now we want to know what actually happened in between. Answers to these questions allow us to further refine our intervention approaches so as to capitalize on the elements with greatest impact, potentially contributing to greater parsimony and specificity as well as opportunities to amplify the "active ingredients" that matter most in the interventions we deliver. Findings of these types can be important to providers and policy makers when making decisions about program funding and investments in future interventions.

Mediators and Moderators

We want to know more about *mediators* of the change process: those processes or events stimulated by the intervention that then lead to and actually cause a portion of the changes measured by intervention outcomes (Kazdin & Nock, 2003) or, in other words, variables during or following an intervention that help explain the mechanisms through which the interventions affect the outcomes (see, e.g., Engstrom, El-Bassel, Go, & Gilbert, 2008; Zweben et al., 2008). An example might be an aversive aspect of the intervention experience that contributes to lower attendance rates among clients, which in turn has a negative impact on the intensity of outcomes achieved (i.e., attendance becomes a mediator).

Several factors that appear to mediate substance use outcomes of individual-level behavioral interventions include client self-efficacy, client adherence to a treatment protocol or treatment plan, the dose of intervention actually received, duration or time span of engagement with an intervention program, individuals' expectancies about the treatment approach engaged, individuals' motivation for treatment and change, the quality of the client–practitioner therapeutic alliance, and treatment engagement. In Figure 2.1, a mediated relationship is said to be present when path A is initially significant and when the addition of the mediator variable results in significance for paths B and C accompanied by a reduction or elimination of the path A significance (see, e.g., MacKinnon, Fairchild, & Fritz, 2007).

Moderators, by contrast, are characteristics, factors, or conditions associated with the influence that an independent variable or intervention has on the dependent, observed outcome variable (Kazdin & Nock, 2003; Kraemer, Kiernan, Essex, & Kupfer, 2008). In other words, the direction or strength of an observed relationship between intervention and outcome variables might be affected by a moderator variable, but the moderator is not being influenced by the intervention variables. For example, a brief intervention for reducing substance use might be significantly and positively effective for individuals with initial mild-to moderate-level substance-related screening scores but not for those with initial screening scores in the severe range. Examples of moderator variables might include traits of the different populations exposed to

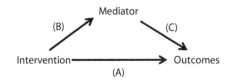

Figure 2.1 Diagrammatic Representation of Mediators as Mechanisms of Change.

the intervention, such as their age, gender, ethnicity, sexual orientation, diagnostic classification, initial symptom severity, or a specific genotype. Generally speaking, the presence of moderation is confirmed by finding a significant interaction between the hypothesized moderator and the independent variable which has demonstrated an effect on an outcome variable (see, e.g., www.davidakenny.net/cm/moderation.htm).

A number of scholars provide guidelines for mediation analysis and designing studies to examine full and partial mediation between specific interventions and observed outcomes (e.g., Baron & Kenny, 1986; Bauer, Preacher, & Gil, 2006; MacKinnon, 2012; MacKinnon & Fairchild, 2009; MacKinnon et al., 2007). We may also be interested in comparing how well our mediation models apply across different subgroups of the population—what we might call "moderated mediation"—and need to apply appropriate integrated analytic approaches to the problem, such as structural equation modeling rather than using "piecemeal" analytic strategies (Bauer et al., 2006; Sidora-Arcoleo & McClain, 2012). Finally, social work investigators may wish to consider the potential influence of suppressor variables: those which correlate with other independent variables and improve the overall predictive power of a tested model by suppressing "outcome-irrelevant" variation among predictors (Pandey & Elliott, 2010).

The Importance of Context
In addition to looking at elements of interventions that are associated with change outcomes, mechanism of change scholars are beginning to address questions concerning the factors that form a context for intervention. As much as elements of an intervention and its dosage as delivered are important, so are facets of the context in which the intervention is received. For example, it is quite likely that a person's response to an alcohol use disorder intervention will be influenced, at least to some degree, by past experiences with treatment or self-change efforts and the

cumulative successes and failures at change over time (Begun, Berger, & Salm Ward, 2011; DiClemente, 2006). Or, for example, does it matter whether or not clients in substance treatment programs are there on a voluntary basis (e.g., Burke & Gregoire, 2007; Gregoire & Burke, 2004; Schaub et al., 2010)? Preintervention contextual variables appear to be related to practitioner and organizational change outcomes with substance intervention training programs as well (Steele-Johnson, Narayan, Delgado, & Cole, 2010). Furthermore, evidence suggests that clients' rate of engaging in treatment after making an initial treatment inquiry is considerably influenced by program-level context factors, such as how complicated the intake processes are, the design of telephone systems, and the "receptiveness" of the reception staff (Hoffman et al., 2011).

Change Outside of Intervention

A related set of questions concerns changes that occur outside of interventions: How do some people "get better" without formal treatment at all, and what happens between intervention sessions? Evidence indicates that some individuals are able to achieve their desired recovery goals without engaging in formal interventions, and various terms have been applied to describe aspects of this phenomenon: *self-change, natural recovery, spontaneous recovery,* and *spontaneous remission,* for example (Bischof, Rumpf, Meyers, Hapke, & John, 2005; Sobell et al., 2002; Tucker & Simpson, 2011; Walters, 2000). Preferable to terminology involving the "spontaneous" recovery notion are terms that maintain an indication of the immense effort that might be involved with change and recovery, with or without professional intervention.

Questions that investigators have asked include whether or not such a thing as "natural recovery" exists, how common it might be, and under what conditions it does or does not happen. The literature suggests that among individuals who exhibit risky drinking patterns, 66–75% revert to either stable, moderate, or abstinent patterns naturally, without formal treatment (Tucker & Simpson, 2011). The picture is less clear among individuals with more severe alcohol problems or those involved with substances other than alcohol. In general, we know relatively little about these self-changing individuals and the processes or factors that contribute to their successful outcomes. A significant implication for social workers investigating substance use topics is the importance of considering whether they are going to look at what happens with interventions or with an individual's change attempts: These may not be interchangeable constructs.

Secondary Data

Much of this chapter centers around activities associated with study design and collection of primary data. A primary data collection strategy affords the investigator many advantages. Among these are the ability to select measures, design an appropriate sampling plan, target data collection to the population, and select data collection intervals that are most appropriate for answering the investigator's research questions. But, primary data collection also has its challenges, such as high costs associated with recruiting and retaining study participants, purchasing permission to use measures that are not in the public domain, and the time involved with data collection activities.

Working with secondary data represents a viable option for answering many research questions, one that may be less expensive and time-intensive than primary data collection. Secondary data sets are those that were collected by another investigator to answer research questions designed by that research team for that study's specific aims. In addition, local, state, and federal government units often collect data to describe the statistical characteristics of particular populations (Boslaugh, 2007); the US Census data represent a good example.

Conducting analyses with secondary data has a number of advantages related to the data having already been collected. Significant costs associated with implementing the study have been borne by the investigator who or the agencies that conducted the original study. Furthermore, with secondary data sets the data have typically been cleaned and adjustments for missing data have been implemented. In many cases these data may have been collected under far more sophisticated sampling strategies than a primary data study could afford to implement, allowing for greater statistical power and stronger generalizations.

There are, of course, disadvantages to employing secondary data. It is unlikely that the data collected specifically apply to the new intended purpose, so there may be key variables for which data are not available, where proxy variables must be identified. When employing secondary data, the investigator is limited to the measures, populations, regions, and time frames selected by the original investigators. Another potential drawback with large national data sets may be the inability to make regional estimates or estimates within subsets of the population. For example, if the research questions are concerned with a group or locale that has low representation in the larger study, then you are likely to find very broad confidence intervals, making statistically significant findings hard to come by. It is also important to remember that data sets that include complex samples and weighting must be analyzed using statistical software that accounts for the characteristics of the sample in order to obtain valid results (Hahs-Vaughn, 2006).

Administrative data are another source of previously collected data that can be used to conduct original research. We distinguish administrative from secondary data primarily as a function of the intent of the original data collection. While secondary data were created to study predetermined research questions, administrative data exist primarily to fulfill organizational and administrative functions, such as billing and reimbursement or reporting to licensing authorities. Examples might include admission and discharge data, birth records, graduation statistics, and clinical practice records. Administrative data sets can be quite large, and significant computing power to access sophisticated data bases may be required, such as in the case of state-wide Medicaid reimbursement data or child welfare information systems. These data sets also can be rather small, specific to a single agency, and contained in a simple spreadsheet.

Generally, the challenges described above with regard to secondary data are magnified with administrative data. The level of rigor typically applied to the collection of primary data for research purposes rarely exists in administrative data sets. Many investigators have been disappointed to learn that very promising variables in administrative data sets were largely missing or entered with a high error rate because they were not directly related to the principal administrative function (e.g., billing) and few controls existed in monitoring during data entry. Staff entering data may not have been adequately trained to avoid systematic data-coding errors. Administrative data require considerably more effort in data cleaning and the construction of study variable indices. Furthermore, the data are representative of only those persons who encountered the service being studied, thereby limiting generalizability to a larger population. However, administrative data sets are widely employed in substance use research and can be a very rich source of data for exploring many important research questions. Epstein's (2010) *Clinical Data Mining: Integrating Practice and Research* is a useful guide for accessing and manipulating existing practice data in order to answer research questions.

In addition to considering the major substance use studies identified earlier as potential sources for secondary data in substance use research, investigators may wish to explore the Interuniversity Consortium for Political and Social Research (ICPSR), which maintains a library of downloadable data sets accompanied by detailed descriptions of how and when the data were collected. Furthermore, many research studies funded by any of the institutes at the National Institutes of Health and National Science Foundation are expected to develop and implement plans for deidentified data sharing at the conclusion of the original study period. Investigators will need to explore their own institution's guidelines for conducting research that utilizes secondary and administrative data sources, particularly with regard to policies for the protection of personal information (e.g., institutional review board, Health Insurance Portability and Accountability Act, and Family Educational Rights and Privacy Act). As a final note regarding secondary data studies, it has been our experience that many first-time investigators vastly underestimate the amount of time it takes to prepare the data set in order to address their particular questions.

PART III: SUBSTANCE USE STUDY VARIABLES

A considerable number and range of variables have been incorporated into substance use studies. This is not surprising as the theories and models driving variable selection are many and diverse. We have options at all levels of measurement, from the intraindividual to those at the interpersonal, family, group, and larger social systems levels (e.g., neighborhood, community, organization, county, state, national, and international).

Before examining specific variables, however, we discuss an important issue to consider when selecting variables for substance use research studies: clinical versus statistical significance. Statistical significance is exciting because it implies that an observed phenomenon is probably not due to chance. For example, following a specific intervention we may see that the average amount of alcohol consumed by the treatment group on a daily basis dropped from 18 to 16 drinks per day, and the difference is significant at the p <.001 level. This may not have a great deal of clinical utility, however, as the average remains in the high-risk drinking category.

In their review of the literature, Cisler, Kowalchuk, Saunders, Zweben, and Trinh (2005) concluded that simply relying on inferential statistics to evaluate the efficacy of interventions is problematic. In part, this is because the statistics are based on aggregate data; what is clinically significant to practitioners and study participants is what happened at the individual level. They summarized the work of several scholars when they described criteria for clinical significance that differ from what investigators might consider for statistical significance, including movement across a functional/dysfunctional threshold rather than changes in outcome score values. For example, a statistically significant 10-point difference on an outcome measure may be clinically significant if those 10 points reflect a difference between poor and good quality of life; the same statistically significant 10 points may be clinically insignificant if the person remains within a category reflecting poor quality of life. The authors recommend greater utilization of clinical significance analysis methods in addiction treatment studies and present a detailed example of how it was performed using the Project MATCH data set (Cisler et al., 2005). Secondary quality-of-life gains related to alcohol treatment may also warrant study attention (Locastro et al., 2009).

Variables to Consider

Making a determination of treatment outcomes simply on the basis of assessing alcohol and other substance consumption is an overlimiting approach and not reflective of much of the current thinking in assessing addiction outcomes (Tiffany, Friedman, Greenfield, Hasin, & Jackson, 2012). Problems co-occurring with substance use are so prominent and pervasive that they may well be the norm rather than the exception (Miller & Miller, 2009). And if addiction is understood as a chronic rather than an acute disorder, outcome measures such as permanent abstinence are probably not realistic indicators of intervention impact (McLellan, 2010; McLellan et al., 2002).

A powerful resource to consider is the report on indicators useful in monitoring alcohol and other substance use produced by the World

Health Organization (2010). The variable categories included in that report help organize thinking about substance use variables. The categories include indicators of alcohol and drug consumption (quantity and frequency rates), alcohol- and drug-related harm, substance treatment, and policy indicators. The report distinguishes between indicators that are at the core of monitoring activities and those indicators considered to be "expanded" in that they complement the core indicators or are "additional" as they may be of emerging or more localized interest.

Quantity and Frequency Variables Related to Substance Use
Many studies incorporate variables about specific types of substances that an individual may have (mis)used. Study variables may also reflect some aspect of "dosage," such as indications of quantity and frequency of consumption for each substance. Quantity and frequency variables have appeared both as independent (predictor) and as dependent (outcome) variables in various studies. Relatively recent guidelines have emerged for the systematic measurement of quantity and frequency of alcohol consumption, resulting in the creation of "standard drink equivalent" formulas; in the United States these are based on ethyl alcohol concentrations of 0.6 oz. of ethanol (see http://pubs.niaaa.nih.gov/publications/ Practitioner/PocketGuide/pocket.pdf). Hence, in the standard drink equivalency examples presented in Table 2.3, one 12 oz. beer (5% alcohol), 5 oz. of wine (12% alcohol), and 1.5 oz. of 80-proof distilled spirits (40% alcohol) are treated as equivalent.

To estimate a drink's equivalence, it is helpful to know that the "proof" figure is easily translated into the percent alcohol by volume: For the United States the proof value is twice the percent of alcohol. Thus, an American beverage that is 80-proof is 40% alcohol by volume. It is a relatively simple matter of computing the drink equivalency ratio. Several interactive Web sites provide reasonably accurate standard drink equivalent computations; it is critical that users pay careful attention to the nationality and units of measure though as the computations and units of measure vary between the United States, the United Kingdom, and other nations (e.g., see www.cleavebooks.co.uk/scol/ccalcoh3.htm). If hand calculating, the formula first involves taking the percent alcohol by volume figure for a beverage and converting the percentage to a decimal (divide the percent alcohol by 100%). Second, dividing the resulting decimal by 0.6 oz. (the amount of pure ethanol in a US standard drink)

Table 2.3 Examples of Standard Drink Equivalence Computations

Reported by Participant	Resulting Standard Drink Equivalents
12 oz. beer (5% alcohol)	1 drink equivalent
5 oz. wine (12% alcohol)	1 drink equivalent
1.5 oz. 80-proof spirits (40% alcohol)	1 drink equivalent
40 oz. malt liquor (7% alcohol)	4.7 drink equivalents
1 25 oz. bottle wine (12% alcohol)	5 drink equivalents
One-fifth of vodka = 25 oz. (40% alcohol)	16.7 drink equivalents
"Hurricane" with 4 oz. of 40% alcohol	2.67 drink equivalents
1.5 oz. overproof rum 75% alcohol	1.88 drink equivalents

obtains the amount of ethanol in each ounce of the beverage. The final step is to multiply this figure by the amount in US ounces of the beverage consumed. In a mathematical formula, computation of standard drink equivalents (*sde*) looks like this in US measures:

$$sde = [(\% \text{ alcohol}/100\%) \div 0.6 \text{ oz.}] \times \text{ounces of beverage consumed}$$

Within this realm of variables, the study of alcohol use is complicated by the need for consistent definitions of constructs such as patterns that reflect "moderation," "binge," "heavy," and "risky" drinking behaviors. The US Department of Agriculture Dietary Guidelines offer a definition of "moderation" in drinking (see www.health.gov/DIETARYGUIDELINES/ dga2005/document/html/chapter9.htm and NIAAA FAQs at http://www. niaaa.nih.gov/FAQs/General-English/Pages/default.aspx#experience). These guidelines are based on epidemiologic evidence concerning increased health risks associated with drinking at higher levels (e.g., liver cirrhosis, inflammation of the pancreas, heart or brain damage, motor vehicle accidents and other injuries, high blood pressure, stroke, violence, some forms of cancer, suicide). For example, adult men up to the age of 60 are advised to drink no more than two standard drink equivalents per day, with no more than 14 per week, and to take at least one day off per week where there is no drinking. For women and for men over the age of 60 these amounts are revised downward to no more than one standard drink equivalent per day and no more than 7 per week. These guidelines, however, specifically exclude individuals who have a problem with controlling their drinking as well as individuals engaging in work or activities where alcohol impairment would be dangerous to themselves or the public, children and adolescents, pregnant women, and individuals taking certain medications that react badly in combination with alcohol; individuals in these categories are advised not to drink alcohol at all.

Binge drinking has been defined often in terms of specific amounts consumed within a specific time frame and more recently in terms of alcohol consumption patterns resulting in specific blood alcohol levels (Fillmore & Jude, 2011). Quantity/frequency definitions often specify five or more drinks in a single drinking occasion (four for women). Outcome criteria typically specify alcohol consumption that produces a blood alcohol concentration (BAC) of 0.08% (gram percent) or more, a rate of consumption that significantly outpaces the body's rate of alcohol metabolism, hence the rise in blood alcohol level. This latter definition is more responsive to the host of factors that influence blood alcohol level within and between individuals, whereas the former may be easier for individuals to recall and record. Neither, it seems, is a perfect indicator of the risk level associated with the drinking pattern (Fillmore & Jude, 2011). The World Health Organization's (2010) report provides additional definitions of patterns, such as heavy episodic drinking, very heavy drinking, and population-level "per capita" consumption rates, along with patterns of drug use. As discussed in chapter 1, variables related to mechanisms of administration may be relevant to many substances of abuse as well.

Symptoms and Diagnosis

Distinctions between substance *use* and *misuse* may be somewhat ambiguous and fluid across studies; *misuse* typically implies use under circumstances of health or other risk, including use that is illegal because of a person's age, where the substances are used, and/or the illegal nature of the substance or how it was procured. Distinctions between *misuse* and *abuse* are more clearly made in the clinical and research literature as the terms *abuse* and *dependence* invoke distinct diagnostic criteria (prior to the 2013 publication of the American Psychiatric Association's *Diagnostic and Statistical Manual of Mental Disorders*, fifth edition [DSM-5], where the terms *substance use disorder* and *addiction* are diagnostically applied). Regardless of the current diagnostic system in use, it is important when working with secondary or longitudinal data to be cognizant of the fact that the data may have been collected under different diagnostic standards.

There are several classic diagnostic schedules employed in substance abuse research. The first of these is outlined in the American Psychiatric

Association's *Diagnostic and Statistical Manual of Mental Disorders,* fourth edition, Text Revision (DSM-IV-TR; 2000), which was the standard applied in many studies up until the 2013 release of the DSM-5 (American Psychiatric Association, 2013). Crucial aspects of diagnosing abuse and dependence are outlined in an overview by Maisto, McKay, and Tiffany (2004), with *abuse* being categorically distinguished from *dependence,* as opposed to *abuse* and *dependence* falling on a single continuum. The defining criteria for an abuse diagnosis applying DSM-IV-TR criteria include

- failure to fulfill major role obligations due to use
- recurrent use in hazardous situations
- recurrent use-related legal problems
- continued use despite experiencing persistent or recurrent problems (social or interpersonal) related to use
- the symptoms have never met criteria for dependence

Criteria for a dependence diagnosis involve three of more of the following occurring at any time during the same 12-month period:

- tolerance
- withdrawal syndrome
- impaired control over one's use
- interference with/neglect of important social, occupational, and recreational activities because of use
- excessive amount of time spent in use-related activities (acquiring, using, recovering from use)
- continued use despite knowledge of recurrent or persistent problems (physical or psychological) caused or exacerbated by use

In the United States, the DSM-IV has been the scheme most commonly utilized in practice and research. There are parallels between it and the *International Statistical Classification of Diseases and Related Health Problems* (ICD-10) system (see the World Health Organization's Web site for the 2010 version at http://apps.who.int/classifications/icd10/browse/2010/en). The ICD-10 system distinguishes between health consequences of acute intoxication, harmful use, dependence, withdrawal, substance (or withdrawal)–induced psychotic disorders including dementia (acute, residual, or late-onset), and substance-induced amnesia.

In May 2013, the fifth edition of the DSM was released by the American Psychiatric Association. Based on reviewing decades of research evidence, the manual's authors determined that it was important to redefine the criteria regarding what does or does not constitute a substance use disorder. In many cases, the revised DSM-5 criteria more closely align with the ICD system; the extent of alignment has important implications for cross-national research. In addition, the new criteria revert to a system by which substance use disorders (SUDs) are classified on a single 11-item continuum of severity, as opposed to the DSM-IV-TR distinction between abuse and dependence on a substance outlined above.

In the DSM-5, the number of criteria met by an individual determines the level of severity for the substance use disorder: no or one criterion does not lead to a substance use disorder diagnosis, "mild" is assigned to the diagnosis based on two or three criteria, four or five criteria lead to a "moderate" SUD diagnosis, and meeting six or more of the criteria leads to a "severe" SUD diagnosis. These categories have important implications for both practice and research studies; for example, it is likely that person with differing levels of diagnosis will respond differentially to specific forms and intensities of intervention. This approach also represents a move from a categorical view (no disorder, abuse, and dependence) to a continuous or dimensional view (no disorder to mild, moderate, or severe disorder).

Greater distinction is made between types of substances involved in a person's substance use disorder with the DSM-5 than was present in earlier diagnostic criteria. Another notable change with the new DSM-5 criteria is the inclusion of *behavioral addictions*, or specific addictions that do not directly involve substances of abuse, such as gambling. There remains debate concerning which forms of behavior may constitute "addictive" behaviors as opposed to compulsive behaviors, such as Internet gaming-, sex-, and food-related behaviors. More details comparing the DSM-IV-TR and DSM-5 are available at sites such as http://www.dsm5. org/proposedrevision/Pages/SubstanceUseandAddictiveDisorders.aspx and http://www.ncadd.org/index.php/get-help/addiction-medicine/ 482-dsm-5-coming-may-2013.

Although the DSM-5 proffers to advance our understanding of diagnosing and classifying mental illness, including substance use disorders, it is not without criticism. For example, concurrent with the DSM-5 being released, the National Institute of Mental Health (NIMH) announced an intention to move away from the DSM classification system in funding research. In issuing their statement, the NIMH suggested that the DSM's categories lacked evidence of validity and that many diagnostic categories were too broad and too often overlooked less common disorders by clustering symptoms. The NIMH was also critical of the use of consensus to determine the diagnostic categories, rather than the use of more objective measures such as neuroimaging and biological measures.

At the time of this writing, the NIMH had proposed funding research under an alternative classification system. Its research domain criteria, while still under development, are built upon three principles: (1) the criteria view mental health disorders as occurring along a continuum from normal to abnormal, rather than imposing categorical diagnostic criteria; (2) the system will eschew current consensus-based diagnostic categories, seeking instead to create classifications based on more objective biometric and neuroscience data; and (3) the criteria will define research constructs from a number of potential units of analysis, ranging from genetic analysis and neuroscience imaging to observed behavior and self-report of symptoms (see http://www.nimh.nih.gov/research-priorities/rdoc/nimh-research-domain-criteria-rdoc.shtml#toc_background). As the principal federal funding agency for mental health research, this is a significant decision and one that has the potential to alter how investigators define problems in mental health and substance use research.

Diagnostic variables of interest may be dichotomous with regard to whether or not an individual meets the criteria threshold for a specific diagnosis or may reflect symptom severity by treating the diagnostic criteria as more continuous variables instead (e.g., degree to which control over use is lost rather than whether or not control is lost, extent of tolerance or withdrawal symptoms rather than their presence or absence, actual number of symptom categories exhibited). As a result of the changes presented in the DSM-5, it is likely that many existing measurement tools and protocols will need to be revised and retested for validity and reliability in both clinical and research applications.

Finally, outside of their application as diagnostic criteria, we might wish to consider variables associated with substance use–related constructs. For example, some investigators are specifically interested in the construct of craving related to substance use (e.g., Lowman, Hunt, Litten,

& Drummond, 2000; Sayette et al., 2000). Others are interested in the closely related construct of temptation (e.g., Harrington et al., 2011). And significant issues related to addiction symptoms also involve dual diagnosis of substance use disorders and mental health conditions, comorbid substance use and physical health conditions, and co-occurring problems with substance use, such as family or community violence, homelessness, and incarceration (e.g., DiNitto, Webb, & Rubin, 2002; Kail, 2010; Moore, 2005; Mertens et al., 2008).

Severity and Consequences

Another important area in describing the experience of addiction and the potential impact of treatment is the level of severity of the disorder and any associated consequences. There are a number of reasons for incorporating these types of data into a substance use research study. Outcome trajectories for persons with substance use disorders vary considerably and often as a function of the disorder's severity (Klein, di Menza, Arfken, & Schuster, 2002; Rosenberg, 1993). Accounting for the influence of severity and other client characteristics upon subsequent outcomes is often an important analytic strategy. Many studies are enhanced by both pre- and postintervention assessments of the disorder's severity, along with its psychosocial consequences. These are important as they provide a potential statistical control but also the opportunity to further inform the literature on matching interventions to client characteristics.

Important research questions exist in furthering the understanding of the prevalence of particular consequences and the ability of interventions to prevent or reduce their impact. It is the consequences of alcohol and other drug misuse that generate much of the societal concern for their use, and as such, their prevalence and response to treatment are good candidates for study (Tiffany et al., 2012). Harm-reduction interventions in particular are specifically targeted at reducing the consequences of substance misuse. Consequences may be significant in a number of life domains, including negative impact on employment or housing status, financial well-being, experiences with the child welfare or criminal justice system, needing health or mental health services, social relations, and psychological functioning. Depending on the analytic strategy to be employed, consequences may be measured as categorical variables (e.g., securely housed, marginally housed, homeless) or continuously (e.g., number of days without secure housing in a given time period).

Typologies and Heterogeneity

As we have suggested elsewhere, addiction is best understood as a multifaceted disorder with varying etiologies and developmental courses of progression and as a disorder that is highly influenced by a variety of biopsychosocial factors. Recognizing this heterogeneity, there is an ample literature describing subtypes of addiction, and their relationship to many outcomes of interest. The DSM-IV criteria for alcohol dependence, for example, specify two subtypes of individual: those who evidence physiological dependence through symptoms of tolerance or withdrawal and those who meet diagnostic criteria without evidence of tolerance or withdrawal (see Maisto et al., 2004) (see Boxes 2.1 and 2.2).

Studies in this area have described empirical relationships between alcoholism typology and both treatment prognosis and treatment outcomes (Babor et al., 1992; Bogenschutz, Tonigan, & Pettinati, 2009; Gregoire, 1996; Kogoj et al., 2010; Thurstin & Alfano, 1988; Zivich, 1981). Others have demonstrated differences by typology in self-efficacy for abstinence (Bogenschutz, Tonigan, & Miller, 2006), level of craving during detoxification, complications during withdrawal (Hillemacher et al., 2006), pharmacotherapy effectiveness (Bogenschutz et al., 2009; Keifer, Jimenez-Arriero, Klein, Diehl, & Rubio, 2007), and at the level of neurobiology (Bierman et al., 2009). Findings that addiction typology has the potential to moderate the trajectory and outcomes of persons with addiction disorders and that subtypes may respond differently to interventions make it important to incorporate information regarding the potential heterogeneity of the population when collecting and analyzing data. In

---

Box 2.1 What Is Tolerance?

Tolerance to a substance is said to have developed when, after repeated exposure to that substance, the effects of exposure diminish. In essence, an individual will need increasingly higher doses (or more frequent administration of the substance) in order to experience the same effects as earlier administrations produced. Tolerance can occur with prescription medications, alcohol, and other drugs of abuse and is largely the result of adjustments in the body to the chronic presence of the substance. Some individuals start out with higher levels of initial metabolic or "functional" tolerance to a substance, rather than or in addition to the acquired form of tolerance.

Box 2.2 What Is Withdrawal?

Withdrawal refers to a set of symptoms that an individual might experience with cessation of or significantly reduced exposure to a substance that has been repeatedly used in the past. It can happen with prescription medications, alcohol, and other drugs of abuse. Acute physical withdrawal symptoms may include effects on the heart (racing, palpitations, tightness in the chest, heart attack), profuse sweating, difficulty breathing, gastrointestinal effects (nausea, vomiting, diarrhea), tremors, seizures, stroke, hallucinations, and delirium tremens. These life-threatening withdrawal conditions are associated with certain substances: alcohol, opioids, and other depressants. (Newborn abstinence syndrome, or NAS, is observed in many neonates as they experience postpartum withdrawal from substances to which they may have been exposed in utero.) Disturbing but less dangerous symptoms are related to many other substances. Psychological withdrawal symptoms may include anxiety, insomnia, irritability, restlessness, disorders of mood/affect, and difficulties with concentration and attention. It is not entirely clear how much of the tolerance and withdrawal experiences are dictated by the pharmacokinetics of the substances involved or the result of learned responses and paired associations to these substances (see Siegel, 2005). Acute withdrawal symptoms may last days to weeks following cessation of the specific substances involved. Individuals may attempt to self-manage withdrawal by taking the same or a similar substance to relieve symptoms.

---

fact, Bogenschutz et al. (2006) argued, "Given the systematic differences between types with respect to dependence severity, consequences, psychopathology, and genetic load, it is not reasonable to assume that the mechanisms of change are constant across types" (p. 563).

Scholars began advancing conceptual models of alcoholism and proposing different interventions and prognoses based on subtype in the 19th century. Many of these early subtypes were distinguished by a single variable, such as age at onset or family history (Gregoire, 1996). In the mid-1980s scholars began developing empirical models that tended to be multidimensional. The well-researched typology presented by Babor et al. (1992) considered four dimensions: premorbid risk factors, pathological use of alcohol and other substances, the level of both chronicity and consequences of alcohol use, and the presence of psychiatric symptoms. From these dimensions two distinctive types of alcoholics (A and B) were derived, differing on the dimensions of age at onset, severity of the substance use disorder, psychological dysfunction, other substance misuse, and the severity of consequences of alcohol and other drug use. Features of type A alcoholism included a later age at onset, less comorbid psychopathology, and fewer behavioral problems during childhood compared to persons with type B alcoholism, who were more likely to have a family history of alcoholism, an early onset, greater chronicity and severity of alcohol-related problems, and more concurrent psychopathology (Babor et. al., 1992). Babor et al. (1992) substantiated the utility of their typology by correctly predicting more severe outcomes for one type; this A/B typology has also been replicated in populations with drug use disorders (Basu, Ball, Feinn, Gelernter, & Kranzler, 2004). Similar subtypes have been demonstrated to exist both across genders and within multiple ethnic groups (Hesselbrock & Hesselbrock, 2006).

Moss, Chen, and Yi (2007) noted that most substance abuse typologies were derived from populations already in treatment for alcohol and/ or drug use disorders. However, they also observed that a high percentage of individuals with addiction disorders never receive treatment. As a result, previous typologies may be representative of only clinical populations rather than the general population of persons experiencing addiction disorders. Employing a latent class analysis with data from the National Epidemiological Survey on Alcohol and Related Conditions, Moss et al. (2007) derived five contemporary subtypes that varied considerably in severity, age, treatment seeking, circumstances under which drinking occurs, consequences of drinking, and other psychosocial functioning factors. Included in this analysis are the following five types that appeared in approximately the following proportions:

- young adult (32%)
- young antisocial (21%)
- functional (19)
- intermediate familial (19%)
- chronic severe (9%)

Many outcome variables of interest have the potential to vary on the basis of the characteristics of both the individual and nature of the addiction disorder. Measuring substance use as a dichotomous variable, recording only its presence or absence, results in the loss of a considerable amount of important information. In doing so, an investigator runs the risk of concluding that the presence of a substance use disorder has no relationship to other outcomes of interest when, in fact, that finding may be a function of an oversimplistic operationalization of substance misuse. The literature on subtypes of addiction disorders introduces the potential for investigating many important research questions, including the potential moderating effect of subtype on intervention access, process, or outcomes as well as the study of efforts to match interventions on the basis on type. However, even in the absence of specific research questions on subtype, it will always be important to heed this literature in constructing measures of what appears to be a heterogeneous disorder.

Symptoms Associated with Quitting

When we work with individuals who abuse substances we also may need to include variables that indicate what happens when a person stops using a substance of abuse. Many of us became familiar with startling news reports of what some victims of Hurricane Katrina and Hurricane Rita endured in the days following collapse of the region's infrastructure. Some of these stories vividly described individuals whose physical and mental health were dependent on psychotropic and seizure disorder prescription medications that suddenly became inaccessible, as well as individuals who lost access to substances like alcohol and "street drugs" for which they had developed physical addictions. This is in light of studies describing high levels of heroin and other opiate treatment needs among addiction treatment–seeking individuals relocated from the areas affected by the two hurricanes compared to non-disaster–affected clients in the system (Maxwell, Podus, & Walsh, 2009). As investigators, it may be prudent to include measures of withdrawal, craving, and other difficult reactions that occur even during intentional quit attempts.

Furthermore, for substance use researchers, being aware of the difficulties involved with distinguishing "symptoms" of withdrawal and early recovery from the symptoms of other disorders is very important. Becoming addicted to a substance involves the body's attempts to achieve normal levels of functioning with the substance present; when the substances are no longer present, the body undergoes a process of establishing new normal levels of functioning once again (Miller et al., 2011). As a result, the recovery process involves a period of acute withdrawal and stabilization but also may require a long-term process of adjustment. The protracted period of adjustment may involve adjustments that affect mood and affect, sleep disruptions, compulsion and craving, cognitive functioning, and relearning of skills that were initially acquired while under the influence of substances (Begun & Brown, 2013). These traits and symptoms may mimic symptoms of various axis I or axis II disorders of mood or personality.

Intervention Outcomes

Intervention outcome variables represent another significant dimension in social work research about substance use. As one possible outcome variable, operationalizing treatment completion might not be as obvious as it seems on the surface. Programs designed in consistently fixed increments or curricula (e.g., 6- or 12-session programs) often lend themselves to a fairly clear definition of services. Programs with more flexible discharge criteria can be considerably more difficult to measure, especially where program staff have difficulty agreeing on the definition of *treatment completion*. When such a variable is measured in these contexts, we have found it helpful to work with program staff to create written checklists of the activities or circumstances that represent a full treatment experience.

While renewed consumption of alcohol or other drugs is an important consideration for assessing treatment outcomes, a thorough determination of individuals' posttreatment functioning must include assessment that extends beyond simply the presence or absence of substance use. Miller (1996) argued that a dichotomous measure consisting of abstinence versus use of substances was overly simplistic and not representative of the recovery trajectories of most individuals. Consider the example from Dennis, Scott, and Funk (2003) where measures of posttreatment outcomes included (1) the number of days of any substance use, (2) the percentage of individuals reporting total abstinence, and (3) the number of days with problems related to substance misuse. Cisler and Zweben (1999) described a composite index for assessing treatment outcome that integrates drinking criteria (abstinence, moderate drinking, heavy drinking) with alcohol-related problems (based on the physical, intrapersonal, social responsibility, interpersonal, and impulse control subscales of the Drinker Inventory of Consequences [DrInC] measure). Similarly, the Addiction Severity Index (McLellan, Cacciola, Alterman, Rikoon, & Carise, 2006) offers a multidimensional approach to measuring an individual's function over the most recent 30 days. The dimensions include personal health (medical and psychiatric) and social functioning (employment, legal, and family/social relationships) domains, along with use of alcohol or other drugs. A topic that has recently been receiving attention concerns how we define *recovery*, both clinically and in research terms. McClellan (2010) offered insight from a panel convened to develop better communication regarding the variable that we might call *recovery*. McClellan indicates the need for a clear, precise distinction between *abstinence* and *sobriety*, which in turn is complicated by confusion regarding the term *sobriety* as meaning either the combination of control, balance, and moderation or complete abstinence. There does seem to be consensus that a person achieves sobriety with reference to all types of substances, not solely to any one type (i.e., alcohol and all nonprescribed drugs). That is to say that someone being treated for a primary problem with cocaine addiction would also be expected to modify his or her use of alcohol and other substances. The discussion becomes muddied, however, when tobacco is involved. Increasingly, substance use treatment programs are viewing tobacco addiction as a primary disorder and incorporating tobacco cessation into treatment protocols (Clark-Hammond & Gregoire, 2011). Another distinction that emerges from McClellan's analysis concerns when a person is defined as being in recovery or having achieved recovery.

A related issue involves the use of medication to assist in maintaining sobriety. The question that arises is whether or not the person has attained the recovery goal if sobriety remains medication-assisted. McClellan's review specifies that the definition of *recovery* is independent from the methods used to attain recovery. The specific example he developed concerns adherence to 12-step principles as the means to recovery but that program adherence does not define recovery per se. While all of this may seem like fine hair-splitting on the surface, it has great import for how investigators measure the construct of recovery. The working definition recommended by the SAMHSA is "a process of change through which individuals improve their health and wellness, live a self-directed life, and strive to reach their full potential" (http://blog.samhsa.gov/2012/03/23/defintion-of-recovery-updated/). This process construct is considerably more difficult to measure than are outcomes.

Another way that outcomes are conceptualized is in terms of time-to-event. We may wish to consider the length of time a person has avoided relapse to use or abuse of substances, given an understanding that lifetime abstinence is an infrequent treatment outcome. As such, assessing the ability of an intervention to delay a return to use is often an appropriate indicator of treatment outcome. An important aspect of these sorts of variables is the definition of *relapse* that is applied. Some investigators use the time when use first starts again; others use the time when use becomes problematic again. This issue is not unlike the more generic problem of using the variable "time" in relation to substance use or addiction: In some cases it is more relevant to examine time elapsed since substances were first used, while in other cases it is preferable to examine when problematic patterns of use emerged or perhaps even the occurrence of consequences such as reincarceration or a return to homelessness.

Intervention Process and Completion

With development of a transtheoretical model of intentional behavior change (e.g., Prochaska, DiClemente, & Norcross, 1992), substance use investigators directed a fair amount of attention to examining how individuals' motivation to change relates to their change attempt or treatment outcomes, including the possibility that intervention strategies may need to be tailored to individuals' orientation to the change process. There are currently a number of ways to measure variables such as treatment readiness and readiness to change as general constructs (e.g., the Readiness Ruler [Hesse, 2006], SOCRATES [Miller & Tonigan, 1996], and the short Readiness to Change questionnaire [Rollnick, Heather, Gold, & Hall, 1992]). Investigators might also be interested in variables related to the model's embedded constructs of self-efficacy for change and decisional balance about change.

Investigators may elect to examine variables related to retention or "dropout" from substance treatment or prevention interventions. Such studies may include factors specific to program participants, program characteristics, or the interaction of participant and program characteristics (see, e.g., Evans, Li, & Hser, 2009; Klein, di Menza, Arfken, & Schuster, 2002). These studies are based on an expanding literature that generally supports the presumption that staying in treatment through completion is associated with better behavioral health outcomes (Comfort, Loverro, & Kaltenbach, 2000; Conners, Grant, Crone, & Whiteside-Mansell, 2006; Milby, Schumacher, Wallace, Freedman, & Vuchinich, 2005; Simpson, Joe, & Broome, 2002; Zarkin, Dunlap, Bray, & Wechsberg, 2002).

Much of the research about treatment retention focuses upon client characteristics, including demographics such as age and race (Choi & Ryan, 2006; Milligan, Nich, & Carroll, 2004), problem severity or comorbidity (Green, Polen, Dickinson, Lynch, & Bennett, 2002; McKellar, Kelly, Harris & Moos, 2006), and pretreatment motivation (Callaghan et al., 2005). However, treatment retention has also been investigated as an interaction of client, provider, and program characteristics. Examples include therapeutic alliance between clients and staff (Marcus, Kashy, Wintdersteen, & Diamond, 2011), interactions between client characteristics and level of staff control (McKellar et al., 2006), and both client and worker responses to programmatic changes (Clark-Hammond & Gregoire, 2011).

Depending on the nature of the program under study, defining *treatment retention* may be very straightforward or present a significant challenge; definitions of *treatment dropout* vary by study (Evans, Li, & Hser, 2009). For programs driven by fixed-calendar treatment protocols, the definition of *dropout* is relatively clear: If a client leaves the program prior to completing, for example, 28 days in residential treatment, he or she can be considered to have dropped out. However, it may be more challenging to determine if and when dropout occurred for clients enrolled in programs without fixed lengths of stay or group interventions with flexible-calendar protocols. Finally, it is worth noting that not all dropouts are client-initiated. Much may be learned by distinguishing between discharges precipitated by clients and those attributed to staff decisions. Clark-Hammond and Gregoire (2011) found an initial increase in staff-initiated termination of clients following a significant programming change and a subsequent increase in client-determined discharges.

Common Factors, Common Elements

After decades of proliferating new constructs and variables in research specific to intervention around substance use disorders, an interesting possibility has begun to emerge: examination of elements and factors related to intervention success that appear in common across studies. *Common elements* are generic aspects that appear across successful intervention strategies as sort of "trans-intervention" ingredients. *Common factors* involve personal and interpersonal characteristics present where interventions have been successful and where these characteristics play a strong role in determining outcomes, perhaps even stronger than components designed to be present in the interventions themselves (Barth et al., 2011). Common factors and common elements are valuable assets as we explore the mechanisms of change involved with substance use disorder interventions (see, e.g., Fraser & Solovey, 2007; Mee-Lee, McLellan, & Miller, 2010).

CHAPTER CONCLUSIONS

Scientific literature on substance use is widely disseminated. There are a number of journals that are specific to alcohol and other drug use disorders. The ubiquitous nature of substance misuse also means that one may find this literature in journals that are not devoted just to substance use studies. In addition, federal agencies such as NIDA, NIAAA, and SAMHSA all provide considerable Web-based resources and information clearinghouses. Finally, systematic reviews of substance use research evidence appear with some frequency in the literature, as well as through the Campbell and Cochrane Collaborations.

An extensive number and range of study designs are available to answer substance-related research questions. While many factors influence the choice of a design and each choice comes with its associated advantages and disadvantages, the research question(s) and status of knowledge development in a topic area should be principal factors in design selection. Controlling for internal and external validity, while critically important aspects of any study, are only part of the picture. Cross-sectional designs, as "snapshots" at a given time, are useful for describing current circumstances associated with substance use. Longitudinal designs incorporate temporal order, which provides the potential for observing change over time; this can include attributing change to interventions. As we are increasingly concerned with how interventions work, we need to pay close attention to issues of intervention fidelity and designing studies that allow for testing the potential roles of mediating and moderating variables in determining how, when, where, and for whom an intervention might be effective.

There are a number of potential variables to consider in designing substance use research; we address their measurement in greater detail in chapter 4. Substance addiction is typically viewed as a chronic condition, which means that measures of length of abstinence, diminished use, and a reduction in harmful consequences may be important outcome indicators. Depending on one's research questions, measures of quantity and frequency of substance use, symptoms of a substance use disorder or withdrawal, and severity and consequences of use may all be important areas of inquiry. Both the trajectory of addiction disorders and their outcomes can vary considerably as a function of typology. The literature provides considerable guidance in this area. Understanding the process of change and the characteristics of those who make change has the potential to make meaningful contributions to understanding what works in substance-related treatment.

3

Participant Recruitment and Retention Practices in Substance Use Research

Studies that fail to recruit and retain sufficient numbers of participants in each "cell" of the design are unable to adequately test hypotheses due to weakened statistical power (Hinshaw et al., 2004; Toerien et al., 2009; Sink & Mvududu, 2010). Furthermore, external validity and study generalizability are seriously threatened if the final sample of participants does not adequately represent the population from which they are supposedly drawn, as a result of either insufficient recruitment efforts or nonrandom study attrition (Braver & Smith, 1996; Ribisl et al., 1996). Historically, this has been a shortcoming associated with much of the research conducted in the area of substance use. For example, we have considerable amounts of data and information concerning individuals who seek and engage in treatment; we know very little about the rest of the population of individuals who use and are addicted to various substances.

Because substance misuse and addiction are fairly stigmatized phenomena (Corrigan, Kuwabara, & O'Shaughnessy, 2009), the population of individuals engaged in or affected by substance use is sometimes difficult to identify, recruit, and retain in research studies. Confounding the issues introduced by stigma are issues related to the effects that the drugs and lifestyle may have on research participation, especially the impact of the behaviors being largely illegal and/or risky in nature. This chapter examines some of the issues and practical tips to improve the quality of social work research by anticipating and addressing many of these difficulties. Contributions from the social work profession are particularly relevant in this chapter because of the profession's rich array of experience in working with client systems immersed in complex, multiproblem circumstances, especially that social workers are familiar with engaging "hard to reach and hard to serve populations," as was noted in chapter 1. The first set of topics that we discuss (Part I) concerns the responsible conduct of substance use research, including human subject research issues that frequently arise in conducting research concerning substance use. In the spirit of avoiding "smash and grab" or "parachute" research, Part I of the chapter also addresses the importance of establishing strong collaborative relationships with agencies and programs and engaging members of the community in advisory capacities before moving too far ahead with study recruitment and retention plans. The final set of topics (Part II) is specific to strategies for enhancing participant recruitment and retention in substance use research studies.

PART I: THE RESPONSIBLE CONDUCT OF SUBSTANCE USE RESEARCH

Research Integrity

Research integrity reflects a number of practices including, but not limited to, utilizing reproducible methodologies, avoiding plagiarism, avoiding/reporting potential conflicts of interest, maintaining responsible collaborative partnerships and working relationships, appropriately engaging in peer review, responsible oversight of data quality and management, responsible and accurate reporting, and ethically involving research participants (see National Academy of Science, 2009). All of these research integrity topics are relevant to substance use research, but here we are focusing on guidelines related to the protection of human research participants. Another report which might be relevant to substance use researchers is specific to research involving the administration of alcohol to study participants, particularly when it includes any populations at risk of or experiencing alcohol use disorders or young, pregnant, or elderly participants (see the National Institute on Alcohol Abuse and Alcoholism report at http://www.niaaa.nih.gov/Resources/ResearchResources/job22.htm).

Policies and Practices to Help Protect Study Participants

The Department of Health and Human Services has established the Code of Federal Regulations related to ensuring the public welfare, Title 45, specifically for the protection of human subjects involved in research, Part 46 (www.hhs.gov/ohrp/policy/ohrpregulations.pdf). Sections of this policy statement explain where, when, and to whom it applies; the organizational structures responsible for research review and oversight (i.e., institutional review boards [IRBs]); and policies, procedures, and criteria for implementing oversight. In the United States, the Office for Human Research Protections directs regulatory oversight procedures for most biomedical and behavioral research related to substance use that involves human participants. Parallel organizational structures to ensure research integrity exist in many other nations as well.

Three guiding principles for the oversight of research involving human participants are derived from the Belmont Report (www.hhs.gov/ohrp/humansubjects/guidance/belmont.html): respect for persons, beneficence, and justice. Every research institution should have a designated office for responsible research practices, including the review of human research as governed by a federal-wide assurance (http://www.hhs.gov/ohrp/assurances/assurances/filasurt.html). Before engaging in any recruitment or data-collection activities involving human participants, all researchers should engage in the research review processes established for their home institution. Most institutional review groups now require study personnel to engage in formal training about the purpose, policies, procedures, and practices in responsible research involving human participants; many institutions are members of the Collaborative Institutional Training Initiative that coordinates this function (www.citiprogram.org).

Collaborative Partnerships

Social work researchers who engage in the study of substance use often have community-based collaborative partnerships with individuals or agencies not covered by a formal IRB with a federal-wide assurance. Depending on the nature of the affiliation between the collaborating institutions, one institution's IRB may be able and willing to assume oversight responsibilities for research-related activities that take place in the partners' agencies or involving the partners' personnel. On the other hand, it may be necessary for the collaborating partners to either (1) develop and certify their own IRB with federal-wide assurance or (2) contract with a private IRB.

Research Involving Protected Populations

Many of the substance use study questions that are important to social work researchers reflect issues surrounding populations that are deemed "vulnerable" in human research terms. Substance use research may involve participants who are (1) prisoners, defined as any individual involuntarily confined or detained in a penal institution; (2) children, defined as anyone who has not attained the legal age for consent; and/or (3) women who are pregnant, their fetuses, and neonates. There are other ways in which individuals involved with substance use might become vulnerable to potential research exploitation or risk suffering negative consequences as a result of participation.

The intersection of substance use and prisoner populations is an important consideration in planning for research in this arena. We know that involvement with the criminal justice system is strongly correlated with substance use: Not only does it often involve illegal behavior but it is also recognized as a *criminogenic* factor—one which contributes to other forms of illegal activities (e.g., Tripodi, Bledsoe, Kim, & Bender, 2011). Epidemiological, etiological, and intervention studies may need to adopt innovative ways of including criminal justice–involved populations (i.e., individuals under supervision in jails, prisons, or communities) in order for the results of their work to be truly representative of the population who use substances and who experience substance use disorders. Prisoner research protections are concerned with ensuring that (1) participants are not subject to undue coercion to participate in a particular study and (2) each individual participant's benefit/risk ratio is appropriate, outside of what benefits may accrue to society from the knowledge developed through the research. These protections are a direct response to historical abuses of prisoner populations in medical and other types of research.

One challenge related to conducting research within a prison, jail, or community-based correctional facility is the ability to maintain confidentiality. These are settings in which privacy and security concerns collide, where participants live in close quarters long after individuals may have shared information with the researchers and where data-collection materials often must be carried in and out through security systems. Another significant prisoner vulnerability challenge relates to intervention studies: There exists a very real potential for disruption of treatment protocols following a participant's release to the community or movement to another facility. Many facilities are also likely to impose constraints on what prisoner research can be conducted because of excess staffing costs associated with supervision and security during intervention or study activities. For example, it can be costly in staff time for prisoners to be escorted or transported to study sites (even within the institution) and to ensure security throughout the facility with outside investigators present.

Concerns that arise with substance use research involving children and pregnant women are centered on ensuring their safety but may also involve issues related to illegal behavior (e.g., underage drinking) and child welfare protection concerns. As mandated reporters, social work researchers need to have detailed action plans in place for how suspected child maltreatment will be handled (including child neglect, endangerment, and substance exposure). They also need to carefully consider how to inform participants about circumstances where mandated reporting priorities could affect research participants' confidentiality assurances. Furthermore, in research involving children, issues arise related to being able to assess their willingness to participate in the research in addition to obtaining parents' consent; this is generally referred to as "participant assent" rather than "consent."

Ethics and Science need to shake hands.

–Richard Clark Cabot

Research Involving Otherwise Vulnerable Populations

In addition to these formally protected groups, some bioethicists advise investigators to consider very carefully the research activities involving other populations whose abilities to protect their own interests may be diminished or compromised (Wendler & Grady, n.d.). This includes individuals with an increased susceptibility to coercion stemming from the fact that they are dependent on receiving treatment from the agencies where the research is being conducted, particularly individuals who lack sufficient resources to seek treatment elsewhere (i.e., receiving care under public assistance provisions, being unemployed or un-/underinsured, or living in a community with few treatment options). This also includes populations who may be vulnerable to exploitation by virtue of their immigration or refugee status and those who come from communities "unfamiliar with modern medical concepts" (CIOMS, 2002).

Individuals whose cognitive abilities are impaired might also fit this description, such as persons with mental illness or those experiencing intellectual/developmental disabilities. These latter groups are possibly more prevalent among potential participants in substance use research than in the general population, indicated by the relatively high rates of psychiatric and cognitive disorders that co-occur with substance use or addiction and because one potential consequence of abusing some substances is short- or long- term impaired cognitive functioning (see chapter 2 for more about cognitive impairment associated with substance use; see also Begun & Brown, 2013). In order to ethically engage these individuals in human research studies, it may be advisable to institute procedures and measures for assessing cognitive competence for providing informed consent as well as to screen for ability to engage meaningfully in the study procedures. When others are engaged to consent on their behalf, investigators should implement strategies for ascertaining the individuals' assent to participate as well.

Equity for Diverse Populations

One way in which the basic ethical principle of justice plays out lies in the equal sharing across population subgroups of any risks and burdens associated with a research study, as well as any potential benefits. In the past, some substance use researchers have systematically and intentionally excluded individuals from their studies based on demographic

We all should know that diversity makes for a rich tapestry, and we must understand that all the threads of the tapestry are equal in value no matter what their color.

–Maya Angelou

characteristics as a means of controlling variability in the studied population. The purposes of the exclusion were either to enhance the internal validity of study findings by reducing heterogeneity or to minimize systematic attrition from a study. A more contemporary philosophy is to ensure the inclusion of representatives of the entire relevant population, especially where external validity, generalizability, and intervention effectiveness (as opposed to efficacy) are research priorities. Social work investigators would be wise to become well versed in ways to make all facets of their research "culturally competent" for the diverse gender, age, ethnic, sexual orientation, religious/spiritual, and diagnostic groups involved: beginning with the research questions being asked and extending through the design, sampling, measurement, analysis, and interpretation activities (e.g., see Marsiglia, Kulis, Rodriguez, Becerra, & Catillo, 2009; Reed & Evans, 2009).

As noted above, one diversity area where substance use researchers encounter significant challenges is the inclusion of participants involved with the criminal justice system. On the one hand, because participant retention is such a crucial facet of valid research, those designing studies need to consider how to handle situations where community-based participants' substance involvement and related activities lead to jail, prison, or other forms of criminal sanction or criminal justice supervision. It may be scientifically irresponsible to simply drop them from the sample but can be very challenging and costly to follow through with them, especially if accommodations were not planned, approved, and implemented prior to an incarceration event. On the other hand, given the high rates at which substance use problems and criminal justice involvement co-occur, social work researchers may wish to devote greater consideration to effectiveness and practice diffusion research that brings approaches with known efficacy into the world of criminal justice systems and persons reentering the community following a period of incarceration.

Incentive Payments

While individuals participate in research studies for a number of reasons (Fry & Dwyer, 2001), the use of modest incentive payments for study participation can encourage both initial enrollment in the study and ongoing participation in the follow-up activities (McKenzie, Peterson Tulsky, Long, Chesney, & Moss, 1999; Meyers, Webb, Frantz, & Randall, 2003; Seddon, 2005). Adolescents, in particular, identify incentives as a significant motivation for participating in follow-up interviewing (Garner, Passetti, Orndorff, & Godley, 2007). However, the nature and amount of research incentives need to be carefully considered: The IRB overseeing the study will have much to say on the matter.

An incentive related to the individuals' time and effort demonstrates respect for their contributions to the project. The function of the incentive is to encourage, but not compel, participation. The incentive amount should be meaningful but modest enough that it does not become coercive to participants, especially those with little means of financial support (McKenzie et al., 1999). It is a delicate balance between incentives that acknowledge a participant's time, efforts, and contributions to knowledge building and incentives that are coercive or encourage someone to participate against his or her own personal interests. Gauging the extent to which any particular amount of incentive payment will be more or less coercive to different populations is difficult and depends on the participants' economic status, age, diagnosis severity, and other factors. One possibility is to calculate a reasonable hourly rate for the average amount of time spent in data-collection activities, then to standardize this amount across all participants.

In addition to the magnitude of the incentive, it is important to consider the type of incentive offered to participants in substance use research studies. As social workers, a strong value is placed on identifying incentive payments that respect participants' rights of self-determination and autonomy in how the incentive is utilized in ways that are personally relevant. Some scholars and practitioners have expressed concern about the use of cash incentives, particularly about providing cash to persons who are at risk of or who have relapsed (see Rush & Morisano, 2010). The concern is that they may elect to use the study incentive to procure alcohol or other drugs or, even more ethically disturbing, that the incentive itself may serve as a trigger to relapse: Money in one's pocket may provide strong temptation for some individuals to drink, buy drugs, party, and/

or gamble; gift cards to certain merchants may be easily traded for alcohol or other substances. Some forms of incentive payment are arguably more likely than others to contribute to relapse or other risky behaviors. However, reviews of the empirical, "expert opinion," and research practice literatures suggest that cash payments have little influence on study participants' subsequent use of substances (Fry, Hall, Ritter, & Jenkinson, 2006; Rush & Morisano, 2010). Conducting focus groups with individuals who could be participants is strongly advised, as is careful monitoring, in studies where there is a potential for this concern to arise. For more specific recommendations, see Fry et al. (2006).

Illegal Behaviors Research

Many behaviors and activities that are studied in conjunction with substance use examine or ask about illegal behaviors, including the use of an illicit substance, misuse of prescription drugs, committing offenses when acquiring substances or while abusing substances, driving while impaired, under-age drinking, or committing any of a number of other potential criminal offenses. As a means of increasing the level of privacy protection for participants in studies regarding the use and effect of alcohol and other drugs, it is highly recommended (and often required by an IRB) that the investigators secure a Certificate of Confidentiality from the various institutes of the National Institutes of Health, the Health Resources and Services Administration, or other Health and Human Services agencies (see http://grants.nih.gov/grants/policy/coc/contacts. htm).

The rationale behind the Certificate of Confidentiality is that it provides an increased measure of protection against "compelled disclosure of identifying information about subjects of biomedical, behavioral, clinical, and other research," which in turn helps investigators achieve the research objectives when data of a sensitive nature are involved (http:// www.hhs.gov/ohrp/policy/certconf.html). This tool is intended to allow investigators to refuse to disclose in civil, criminal, administrative, legislative, or other federal, state, or local proceedings any identifying information about participants in a covered research study.

The Certificate of Confidentiality does not preclude identity disclosure in circumstances related to mandated reporting policies and in response to professional ethics obligations (e.g., social workers' reporting of suspected child abuse or a threat of violence against self or others), and the consent form needs to clearly indicate these reporting responsibilities. The Certificate of Confidentiality is also not a protection against demands for information used for auditing or evaluating federally funded projects or information necessary for meeting federal Food and Drug Administration requirements. Although issued by the National Institutes of Health, federal funding is not a prerequisite for obtaining a Certificate of Confidentiality.

Safety Concerns

Investigators engaged with substance-abusing individuals need to have standard operating procedures in place for managing potential safety risks that may arise. In many instances these standard operating procedures are no different from what many mental health and addiction treatment programs have in place: assessing and managing suicidality, recognizing and responding to medical emergencies frequently encountered with substance use and addiction (e.g., overdose, opioid withdrawal, diabetic and cardiac emergencies), and safety protocols to protect investigative team members and participants. (Related to addressing increased suicidality in substance treatment, see Center for Substance Abuse Treatment, 2009).

One scenario for which it is important to develop safety plans involves what to do when a participant appears to be under the influence of alcohol or other drugs. Aside from potential data-quality concerns, this situation affects a person's ability to effectively engage in the consent process, as well as raising issues of personal and community safety related to their transportation, ability to protect oneself from accidental injury or harm caused by others, and risk of overdose. Another safety-planning issue concerns the physical security of staff and participants when incentives with monetary value are involved, as well as securing the actual incentives from theft. Think through what it might mean for other participants or others in the community to know that incentives are in someone's possession.

Participants in Community-Based Substance Use Research

A first principle in preparing to conduct substance use research begins well before the actual initiation of participant recruitment and retention activities. Successful engagement of members of the community is important in ensuring valid and reliable data collection and analysis. This may mean engaging individuals who are currently abusing substances, engaged in treatment services, recent "graduates" of treatment programs, delivering services or treatment, or otherwise representative of the populations that will be engaged in the study activities. These individuals can serve as consultants who can provide you with a "reality check" concerning the planned recruitment and retention strategies—as well as the planned measurement/data-collection tools and interpreting the study results in meaningful ways. It may be advisable to initiate one or a series of informative focus group sessions with different constituencies during the preplanning period.

It is often crucial to begin the preplanning period by building strong relationships and rapport with agencies, programs, and providers of services to the population of individuals who misuse substances or are affected by others' substance misuse. Providers may eventually become engaged in participant recruitment and even successfully participate in data-collection procedures, but this is not likely if strong, trusting, mutual relationships have not been established first. In order to conduct high-quality substance use research, the time and effort of building and maintaining strong collaborative relationships are important—it is often through the shared experience of a series of increasingly central, cumulative successes over time that these collaborative relationships produce meaningful results (see Begun et al., 2010).

We know that establishing and maintaining relationships characterized by trust, mutual respect, and a collaborative spirit are crucial to being able to engage community members in the research process, particularly when the research involves ethnic minority communities (Armistead et al.; 2004; Hinshaw et al., 2004). These relationship elements are no less critical to research that involves programs, agencies, organizations, or institutions. One strategy that social work investigators may wish to employ involves engaging a program's team members in organizational assessment activities to identify what is "pushing and pulling" for involvement, the extent to which there exists organizational readiness to engage in the research activities, and what will be the mutually satisfying "win–win" aspects of the research relationship. The team might employ one or more brief measures of organizational readiness to change or adopt new behaviors as part of the assessment process (e.g., see chapter 4 as well as Goldman, 2009; Weiner, Amick, & Lee, 2008).

> By mutual confidence and mutual aid—great deeds are done, and great discoveries made.
>
> –Homer

These forms of assessment and relationship building are important when service providers are going to be engaged as sources of referral to research protocols. The providers need to develop their own comfort with and understanding of the potential benefits of research participation for their clients. The assessment processes are essential where the collection, tracking, and reporting of data are to be conducted by service providers. The providers will need training in the recruitment, retention, and research consent procedures involving participants who are also clients being served by their programs; these activities are not necessarily consonant with professional practices related specifically to providing services. Investigators also need to become aware of factors acting at the point of interface between programs and clients as this juncture and the perceived "goodness of fit" with the research-related activities potentially have a tremendous impact on participation (Lee, 2009).

PART II: ENHANCING PARTICIPANT RECRUITMENT AND RETENTION

Significance of the Issue

The soundness of any research study is determined to a very large extent by the adequacy and appropriateness of the sample through which data are derived. Adequacy is multifaceted, including such features as sample size and representativeness. Recruitment activities typically focus on ensuring that adequate numbers and types of participants become enrolled in a particular study. Retention activities typically emphasize maintaining adequate participation of enrolled individuals over the course of the study as designed.

An investigator's ability to develop valid inferences, particularly about intervention efficacy or effectiveness, may depend on the level of success in conducting sequential interviews with a high percentage of the participants originally recruited for a longitudinal, repeated measurement study. Obtaining high follow-up rates is critical in order to maintain the distribution of the original sample and avoid introducing systematic bias.

Sampling Issues

A critical issue that must be addressed early in the planning of a research study involves making an informed determination as to the number of elements about which data will be gathered (e.g., individuals, couples, families, interventionist–client pairs, groups, communities). This issue goes hand in hand with statistical power analysis and estimation of effect sizes in observed group differences. A variety of resources are available to assist social work investigators in determining the numbers of participants needed for a competently executed empirical study. For example, the Dattalo (2008) book provides both a general overview of the issues involved and specific details about implementing the requisite techniques.

Sample size is one of several factors at the investigator's discretion that has an impact on a study's statistical power or ability to minimize the Type II error rate (Kline, 2009). Cohen's d for assessing effect size, a statistical tool to help determine whether or not the magnitude of an observed contrast or difference is meaningful, is dependent on a study's sample size (see Fritz, Morris, & Richler, 2012; LeCroy & Krysik, 2007). Fritz and MacKinnon (2007) argue that it is useful in planning a study, rather than at its conclusion, to know the sample size required for achieving the desired level of power for detecting an effect (e.g., 0.8 with $\alpha = .05$) and that this takes on a special meaning when the study involves mediated effects.

In substance use disorder intervention research, we might also wish to consider applying a "number needed to treat" approach, an indicator of the number of individuals who would need to be treated in order for the treatment response to be better than no treatment or a placebo control group. This measure is a function of the relationship of the probability of continued substance misuse following an intervention for both the intervention and comparison groups. Higher values call into question the efficacy of the intervention as they indicate minimal variability in treatment outcomes as a function of treatment versus comparison group participation.

Additional basic principles and strategies generically related to sampling in research studies are discussed by Kakinami and Conner (2010), who address types of probability and nonprobability sampling in quantitative research as well as sampling approaches for qualitative studies.

Participant Recruitment Activities

Participant recruitment activities have, as their primary goal, enrolling the numbers and types of individuals in the study to meet the design specifications. The formal recruitment process, particularly for intervention studies, can be summarized in four general steps: generating contacts, informing them about the study particulars, screening for eligibility, and study enrollment (Berger, Begun, & Otto-Salaj, 2009). With regard to substance use research, each of these steps can involve unique challenges.

Generating contacts is aimed at identifying potential study participants and attracting their attention to the study in which they will hopefully become enrolled. Social work investigators will need to carefully consider the potential disadvantages of relying too heavily on recruitment strategies that involve traditional and mainstream advertising media—individuals attracted through newspaper advertising, for example, may not be representative of the target population. The use of contemporary social media and technologies may or may not suffer the same threat, depending on age and other demographic characteristics desired in the participant sample. Furthermore, since the research may very well be investigating behaviors that are either illicit or highly stigmatized, contacting potential participants can be challenging. Substance use investigators need to carefully review their initial contact materials from the perspective of the potential participant with regard to how stigmatizing its contents might be, how safe potential participants might be made to feel, the extent to which they might want to associate with or become committed to the study, and the cultural responsiveness of the materials (Berger et al., 2009; Clay, Ellis, Amodeo, Fassler, & Griffin, 2003).

The stigmatizing messages in recruitment materials might seem subtle to an investigator. For example, one aborted study recruited only two families out of a potential pool of 1,500. Investigators advertised through letters hand-delivered by their counselors to individual men and women in treatment for alcohol or other drug-related problems. The letters indicated that the study sought families whose adolescent children were at risk of developing substance use problems by virtue of their parents' substance use. While logically reasoned, the assumptions conveyed through these materials were also very threatening to families struggling with a parents' recovery attempts. Recruitment (and other study) materials should also be free of labels like "substance abuser" or "alcoholic" or "addicts." Throughout this book we have taken great care to use person-centered phrases and terms that describe behaviors rather than labeling people. Initial contact materials may need to be more generically and gently scripted, while still being sufficiently informative about the study.

Investigators may find it necessary to engage person-to-person networks in the initial stages of participant recruitment, particularly in substance use studies, which so often involve hidden populations. According to Miller et al. (2010), hidden populations are comprised of individuals "difficult or impossible to identify using routine sampling methods" (p. 28). Individuals who use substances very often meet the criteria for membership in a hidden population (Miller et al., 2010).

Respondent-driven sampling is a highly specialized, nonprobability sampling strategy which also incorporates systematic network analyses as a means of identifying hidden populations (Salganik & Heckathorn, 2004). In this approach, early enrolling respondents or "seeds" are engaged in recruiting participants from within their own networks through successive recruitment waves until convergence or saturation has evolved—usually within six waves (Heckathorn, 1997). Participants recruited in this manner are linked through network analysis.

In some communities, the population of individuals who use substances is an "overstudied" group; participants are drawn from among those who are most easily located and heavily studied. With many investigators recruiting the same individuals into their study samples, the body of knowledge begins to become skewed around these relatively few, frequent participants. We have heard of "semiprofessional research subjects" in some communities: people who volunteer for many different addiction studies, potentially receiving concurrent interventions. Sometimes members of the network compare incentives for the different studies and hold out for those with the best incentives. In the long run, the field may find itself in a position not unlike what happened with cancer researchers who spent decades all studying the same particularly hardy cell line only to find that, while they knew a lot about that particular cell line, the knowledge did not generalize particularly well to other cancers or even other cell lines within the same form of cancer (see Skloot, 2011). Or, for example, the problem that arose with studying alcohol use disorders among lesbian, gay, bisexual, and transgender men and women by recruiting from gay bars—we know something about individuals who participate in this bar scene but virtually nothing about lesbian, gay, bisexual, and transgender drinking in the rest of the population. In the long run, substance use investigators need to exert considerable amounts of ingenuity and creativity in recruiting across the populations of interest.

Informed Consent Procedures

The informed consent process through which potential participants learn about the study details is an important phase of building a relationship with the project. Investigators would be wise to choreograph the consent process to be engaging while being informative, rather than thinking of it simply as an opportunity to get a consent form signed. Potential participants may be sensitive to the entire atmosphere and experience of the informational and consent procedures, so investigators would be wise to devote considerable attention to how the information is presented and the training of individuals engaging potential participants in the consent process. For example, it might be best to present some of the information pictorially or through video, rather than simply through the written word.

Screening Procedures

Screening is an additional important aspect to plan carefully in substance use research. While it may be important for enhancing participant homogeneity (particularly in efficacy trials), it is also important to recognize the impact of exclusion criteria on overall sample size. The more stringent are the exclusion criteria, the smaller the initial pool of potential participants becomes and the more difficult to enroll the numbers of individuals needed to achieve acceptable study power. Ideally, exclusion criteria are imposed to ensure participant safety (e.g., excluding women who may be pregnant from certain intervention studies) and reliability of the data (e.g., excluding individuals who do not understand the measurement tools or other procedures). Remember that the screening protocol is also an important opportunity to affect potential participants' experience of the research project. Careful attention to factors like the screening environment, measurement burden, and rapport with the person conducting a screening interview matter to participants and influence their willingness to engage in the study.

Random Assignment

Experimental designs to investigate interventions often involve random assignment of participants to different conditions—random assignment is not to be confused with random selection of a sample from a population. The purpose of random assignment is to reduce the potential impact of subsample selection bias on the internal validity of intervention study results. One practical problem with this approach is that it depends entirely on potential participants' willingness to be randomized to any one of the designed conditions. As Dattalo (2010) discusses, a person who enrolls in the study with a strong preference for receiving a particular intervention may drop out of the study if randomized to another condition.

In some cases participants may have suspicions about "truthfulness" in the random assignment process. As a response to this concern, in one of our studies involving random assignment of incarcerated women to intervention versus treatment as usual conditions, we placed colored cards from the game Uno˚ into sealed envelopes in the proportions that we needed to replicate through randomization. The women selected their own card from the stack, thereby determining their own fates, and were generally appeased as to the fairness of the randomization method (see Begun, Rose, LeBel & Teske-Young, 2009).

In other instances, it may be a service provider who is unwilling to support the condition to which a particular participant has been randomized; he or she may have referred a potential participant to the study because he or she wanted the person to receive the experimental or innovative intervention. Dattalo (2010) explores hybrid models of partial randomization that can help manage this sort of situation. Unfortunately, intervention team members may, with the best intentions for a participant, ultimately sabotage the integrity of the random assignment process. One suggestion to prevent this is to ensure that all team members are well informed about the role of random assignment in the "greater good" of the study having methodological integrity. Finally, some statistical alternatives to systematic random assignment have appeared in the literature, such as propensity score matching (e.g., see Dattalo, 2010).

These, however, are not advised as "band-aid" solutions for failed random assignment and require thoughtful attention to their own limitations.

Participant Retention Activities

As noted in chapter 2, studying substance use disorder interventions often involves making multiple longitudinal contacts with study participants, following them during the course of intervention and at multiple postintervention intervals. Participants in substance use studies can be very difficult to track in the community because of the lifestyle that is often attendant with substance misuse and because social networks and life structures can change dramatically in concert with posttreatment functioning (Scott, 2004). A number of studies have observed significant relationships between the level of difficulty in locating study participants and participants' posttreatment functioning. As might be expected, clients who prove to be more difficult to locate are less likely to experience positive intervention outcomes (Scott, 2004; Hansten, Downey, Rosengren, & Donovan, 2000; Sullivan, Rumptz, Campbell, Eby, & Davidson, 1996; Walton, Ramanathan, & Reischl, 1998). This suggests that drawing study conclusions in the presence of lower follow-up rates may result in overstating any identified benefits associated with the studied intervention.

There has been considerable discussion in the literature regarding the minimum follow-up rate necessary to retain confidence in the study findings (Kleschinsky, Bosworth, Nelson, Walsh, & Schaffer, 2009). For example, Hansten et al. (2000) found that a 60% follow-up rate produced a sample that had little or no difference from the same sample when 90–100% of the subjects were located. In contrast, Scott (2004) demonstrated that even a 70% response rate was likely to be significantly biased. A 70% rate is an oft-stated rule of thumb for satisfactory follow-up (Hansten et al., 2000). The Center for Substance Abuse Treatment currently requires a minimum 80% follow-up rate in their funded studies.

While there is no argument that higher rates are preferred, obtaining them is very expensive, absorbing a great deal of effort and long-term commitment of resources. Recent studies have documented a mean of 8.6 participant contact attempts to obtain a 70% follow-up sample (Kleschinsky et al., 2009), 10 attempts for a 75% sample (Walton et al., 1998), and up to 33 contacts to obtain a 90% follow-up rate (Scott, 2004). New investigators often underestimate the costs associated with maintaining acceptable follow-up rates. Meyers et al. (2003) estimated that it took an additional $85 per adolescent participant for each wave of completed interviews in their study. Regardless of the resources available to the investigator, implementing a systematic approach to participant retention will increase the value of the research. Research teams need to plan for the considerable costs associated with implementing a solid retention plan. However, the importance of obtaining high response rates, especially in longitudinal and intervention studies, requires the investigators to make a significant commitment in order for the study to yield meaningful outcomes.

Intent-to-Treat

The intent-to-treat design of classical intervention studies, where all enrolled participants are tracked regardless of whether or not they complete their assigned programs, is an important tool for improving the accuracy with which results are interpreted. Intent-to-treat methodologies introduce significant challenges however, particularly with regard to participant tracking. While tracking program graduates may be challenging, locating and engaging participants who disenroll prematurely can be exceedingly difficult. These studies may be resource-intensive to implement; however, the study findings become far stronger as a result.

Retention Tracking Systems

Adequate participant tracking matters in intervention research. A number of published protocols describe effective strategies for tracking both adults and youth in the community (Scott, 2004; Hall et al., 2003; Sullivan et al., 1996). The initial study enrollment period is the time to collect contact information for each participant. Typical information includes full names and nicknames; e-mail, home, and work addresses; and numbers for home and mobile telephones as well as pagers. With a population of individuals involved with substance use, it is particularly important to include information concerning participants' plans for moving in the near future. In a recent study that involved tracking adolescents in the community, we experimented with collecting social media data, such as Facebook, MySpace, and Twitter accounts. While attention must be paid to confidentiality with social media, activities such as enrolling youth in a restricted Facebook account for the project can be a useful mechanism for staying in touch. Collecting Social

Security and driver's license numbers can also be useful for future tracking activities but increasingly is being discouraged in contemporary identity theft–protection efforts. The enrollment form should obtain extensive contact information for collateral informants. The list of collateral informants should include both the participant's family and social network members, along with his or her social service network. Social network records include detailed contact information similar to that collected about the study participant and should be obtained for at least three family members and/or significant friends/others who the participant identifies as likely to be able to assist in locating him or her during the time frame of the study. Collateral informant lists should also reflect the changing status of social networks: The network in which participants can be located will be largely determined by their recovery condition at follow-up. It is important to gain access to both their "using" and "recovery" networks (Scott, 2004) and to update the list at each subsequent study contact point. In collecting this information, our practice is to affirm and reaffirm for study participants our commitment to preserving confidentiality and to provide them with the script that we follow when contacting collateral informants. That script makes reference only to their participation in a university-sponsored study and avoids disclosing their participation in treatment or other potentially stigmatizing aspects of their study participation. An IRB protocol will most likely need to include such a script as well as a description of the plan to handle the collateral informant information in a secure manner that protects confidentiality.

The appropriate engagement of social service collateral informants will vary extensively, depending on the nature of the study participants and interagency policies. It can be helpful to identify any caseworkers, clinics, food pantries, and religious institutions with which the participant has been engaged, as well as any actively involved probation and parole officers. If a participant has a history or a risk of being homeless, the tracking form should identify shelters and other locations where he or she has stayed or is likely to stay in the future. If the intervention is being delivered by a community agency, it is important to engage the clinicians in supporting tracking and locating efforts. Agency practitioners may view tracking and posttreatment follow-up as being outside their purview; in fact, they can be extremely helpful in locating and reengaging clients to gain intervention outcome knowledge.

The recruitment interview is the time to obtain appropriate releases from participants so that the professional community can be contacted later as needed. (Policy concerning health information privacy and the interface with research can be reviewed at the Health Insurance Portability and Accountability Act site http://www.hhs.gov/ocr/privacy/hipaa/understanding/special/research/index.html). Beyond collecting a release of information to present to the agency, taking the time to form a relationship with key personnel in advance can be beneficial. A release of information may legally entitle the investigator to inquire of a client's whereabouts, but the agency's level of commitment to supporting the tracking effort is more a function of the goodwill formed in advance of an investigator asking for specific assistance. In the presence of a good working relationship, even an agency that declines to provide the investigator with contact information may be willing to forward a letter or make contact on behalf of the investigator.

Maintaining regular contact with participants is important, especially at intervals between data-collection points that are widely spaced (e.g., follow-up data at 12, 24, and 36 months). The appropriate intervals for contact will depend on the population however. For some, a contact every 3 months may suffice, where that contact includes an update of the tracking form. With our recent studies of individuals reentering the community following a period of jail or prison incarceration, it was important to update every 2 weeks during the initial postrelease period. Longitudinal studies have reported that subjects are often lost in the first 3 months after being enrolled (Walton et al., 1998). Depending on the intervention design, there may be opportunities for regular tracking contact with study participants during the course of treatment where there is great benefit in maintaining rapport and regularly updating the tracking form.

Most follow-up protocols establish a window of a few weeks on either side of the scheduled interview date in which to locate and conduct the interview. As that window approaches it is good practice to begin locating and scheduling the interview well in advance of the window opening. This allows considerable time to work through the list of collateral informants if early efforts to locate and schedule are unsuccessful. As Martinez and Wong (2009) attest, attendance in intervention protocols can be enhanced with judicious use of telephoned and written reminders to participants as well.

It is important to maintain a tracking log, such as a spreadsheet or similar database, which displays the follow-up schedule and documents all tracking efforts. Documented tracking efforts might include the type of effort made (mail, phone, text message, etc.), the date and time, and the outcome. When tracking difficulties arise, this log can be valuable in assessing the problem and identifying alternative strategies (e.g., calling later in the day or on a different day of the week). Within budgetary limitations, it is beneficial to establish a wide time frame in which tracking staff are available and to spread contact attempts across that range as clients are sought for interviews. For example, a 7-days-a-week and 15-hour day provides a wide range of calling hours (Scott, 2004). In our study of adolescents in the community we provided project staff with cell phones that would allow them to take calls outside of traditional office hours and prevent staff from having to wait by an office phone for a returned call.

Follow-up rates also increase when effort is given to identifying in advance participants who are at greater risk for being lost to follow-up and adapting strategies to better engage and track that group (Kleschinsky et al., 2009; Zweben, Barrett, Berger, & Tobin Murray, 2005). In general, follow-up is most successful when it includes a somewhat flexible yet systematic approach in terms of providing options for the schedule, the interview method, and the location in which the subject can complete interviews (Kleschinsky et al., 2009; Zweben et al., 2005; Meyers et al., 2003).

When direct and collateral informant contacts are unsuccessful and resources allow, investigators can turn to public record searches in an effort to locate study participants. Having staff search social media Internet sites such as Facebook and MySpace offers another efficient and low-cost staring point. Internet-based fee-for-service providers that search a number of public record databases can also be consulted. Hall et al. (2003) reported that purchasing credit bureau reports can be an effective method for locating someone and suggested that LexisNexis searches of state and federal public records can be fruitful. Many criminal justice records are publically available and increasingly accessible via the Internet. State and federal prisons often have online inmate locator search engines. Use of these tracking resources should be addressed in the IRB protocol, however, and explained in participant consent procedures.

Rapport and Relationship Building

During and following the initial interview, the tracking effort requires building rapport and maintaining regular contact with the participant. A critical dimension to address in planning the retention process is the participants' experience of being engaged in the project, or the *project climate*. Successful retention begins when the participant is first recruited for the research study. The enrollment phase provides an opportunity for the interviewer to begin building rapport, essential to successful tracking and retention (Hall et al., 2003; Fry & Dwyer, 2001).

During initial enrollment it is important to help participants understand both the importance of their participation in the study and the need for their involvement (Scott, 2004). Adult study participants have cited reasons such as altruism and the recognition that they have something to contribute as a reason for participating in research (Fry & Dwyer, 2001). The recruitment strategy should appeal to those motives. In our own studies, individuals who have dropped out of the treatment intervention often indicated that they assumed they were no longer needed in the research aspect of the study or had become ineligible for further data collection.

Providing incentive payments at the beginning of an interview avoids leaving participants with the perception that they must answer every question in order to receive the incentive, can reduce a sense of coercion, and can enhance rapport. Another early-relationship strategy is to send a thank-you note both via electronic and postal e-mail shortly after enrolling the participant. This also serves to verify the provided addresses. A return of either as undeliverable should trigger follow-up action on the part of the research team. We regularly send birthday and holiday cards to study participants through the US mail. This serves the dual purpose of reverifying the contact information and maintaining a relationship with the participant.

While some literature suggests that ease of contact and study retention are often a function of client characteristics and current level of functioning (Claus, Kindleberger, Dugan, 2002; Fry & Dwyer, 2001; Scott, 2004), there is also evidence that interviewer characteristics and subjects' relationships with interviewers influence the study team's ability to locate subjects and complete follow-up interviews (Fry & Dwyer, 2001; Garner et al., 2007). A key interviewer competency to consider in staffing the research team is the ability to build rapport with the participants being followed in the community (McKenzie et al., 1999). Other strategies may include using the same interviewer for each interview across a longitudinal study and matching interviewers to clients on variables such as gender, race, and age (McKenzie et al., 1999). Attention must also be given to which project personnel conduct the follow-up interview. In smaller projects study staff may take on multiple roles. However, the role of the primary treatment provider should not include conducting follow-up interviews. Study participants may be less likely to reveal negative behavior when there is a real or imagined negative sanction associated with doing so. Even in the absence of potential sanction, social desirability bias may influence a participant's willingness to disclose to someone with whom he or she has a therapeutic relationship.

CHAPTER CONCLUSIONS

Participants in substance use research are often vulnerable persons, due to their engagement in potentially illegal, embarrassing, and social unacceptable behavior; human subject research protection efforts may involve attention to several specific issues with which investigators used to working with other populations may be unfamiliar. A specific example involves soliciting and securing a Certificate of Confidentiality as protection against forced disclosure by an investigator, over and above securing approval of procedures by the appropriate certified review board for the protection of human subjects.

It is also important to be mindful of the risks that are associated with the lifestyle under study. Depending on the nature of the study the investigator may need to have provisions for monitoring for symptoms of withdrawal, which can be life-threatening. Child abuse and neglect, family violence, and concomitant health or mental health conditions may be more common among individuals and in families experiencing substance use. The responsible investigator has reflected upon the potential for each given the nature of the current study and has a plan for protecting study participants, securing advice from consultants if necessary.

Studies are improved with broad representation of potential participants. Forming collaborative partnerships with local agencies can significantly improve recruiting efforts, as can strategies that reduce both stigma and fear of disclosure for study participation. It may be helpful to systematically engage study participants in the recruitment of additional participants, particularly when working with potentially hidden populations such as those who are homeless or experiencing heavy burdens of stigma. Many studies employ intent-to-treat models, in which participants are tracked regardless of subsequent study participation. While difficult to implement, such studies are inferentially stronger than those tracking only individuals who complete an entire intervention. There is much to be learned from nonparticipants and those who drop out of intervention studies prematurely. Making valid inferences in any longitudinal study requires retaining a high percentage of study participants. Participants in substance use studies are often particularly difficulty to track, especially when conducting intent-to-treat study models. However, there are well-researched protocols that enable the high retention and follow-up rates required for making valid inference. Engaging with study participants, making use of appropriate incentives, and advance collection and verification of contact data can result in long-term follow-up rates well in excess of 90%.

4

Measurement and Analysis in Substance Use Research

In a discussion concerning the assessment of alcohol problems, Allen and Wilson (2003) describe as "regrettable" an observed failure to utilize formal, validated assessment procedures in clinical and research practices. Their argument is based on an assumption that both practice and research will be improved when assessment measures with demonstrated reliability and validity are utilized. In addition to reliability and validity, we should be concerned about practical application issues. Relative cost and benefit issues for data-collection approaches are closely intertwined with the essentials of data reliability and validity. In this chapter, we examine substance use research issues associated with the collection of data with self-report approaches, data collected from individuals susceptible to substance-related cognitive impairment, measurement involving individuals in controlled settings, and measurement concerns related to persons from diverse backgrounds. We then present and discuss a number of specific measurement tools and approaches that have appeared in the substance use literature, at both the "micro" and "macro" levels.

PRACTICAL ISSUES IN MEASUREMENT

One practical measurement issue revolves around measurement equivalence across populations with regard to the instruments used in substance use research studies. Individual-level measures are most useful when comparative norms are available, especially norms developed specifically for the diverse populations participating in a particular research study. For instance, there exists a considerable body of literature indicating that women's experiences with many substances differ from the experiences of men, from their physiological responses, pathways, and timelines to addiction to some of the associated health risks and responses to certain treatment approaches (National Institute on Alcohol Abuse and Alcoholism, 2011; National Institute on Drug Abuse, 2006; Sun, 2009).

Measurement equivalence across populations is an important consideration in research efforts to address and redress ethnic or racial disparities in the substance use arena (Burlew, Feaster, Brecht, & Hubbard, 2007). Differences in how members of different groups respond to measurement tools may, in some cases, be more reflective of differences in "fit" with or relevance of the measures, rather than actual differences in lived experiences. As a simple example, if individuals are asked to report the number of beers they drank on a particular day, the numbers are not comparable across groups that purchase beer as six-packs of 12 oz. cans versus as 40 oz. bottles. While many instruments are available, their appearance in the literature unfortunately is not always supported by sufficiently tested comparative norms. The Burlew et al. (2007) article outlines statistical approaches that investigators should consider applying in addressing potential sources of measurement nonequivalence in their studies, including assessing the extent to which the factor structure and factor loadings for a particular measure are consistent across groups.

A second topic that follows from measurement equivalence is the establishment of "cut points" or standardized threshold levels for defining research or screening criteria. For example, the Alcohol Use Disorders Identification Test (AUDIT) has traditionally applied criteria whereby scores ≥ 8 meet criteria for classifying a person's drinking pattern as potentially harmful (Babor, Kranzler, & Lauerman, 1989); however, this screening instrument appears to work better for women when the criterion point is lowered to scores ≥ 7 (Bradley, Boyd-Wickizer, Powell,

> Most of the yield from research efforts comes from the coal that is mined while looking for diamonds.
>
> –Paul D. Boyer

& Burman, 1998). Similarly, Cherpitel and Clark (1995) demonstrated that five different screening instruments performed differently with subgroups based on gender and race (black or white). Investigators are advised to consider these issues in substance use measurement selection when criterion points are to be used in participant inclusion/exclusion decisions, as well as in study analyses.

A third general application issue concerns the categorical versus continuous nature of variables measured by a substance use instrument. Researchers who use clinical tools often are faced with the temptation to use participants' actual scores, acting as if the instrument measures a continuous variable. However, many clinical instruments are designed only to classify individuals as being above or below a certain threshold or criterion cut point—in other words, as a dichotomous variable. Depending on the nature of the statistical analyses planned and the way the sample distribution plays out, it may be preferable to work with dichotomous, quartile, quintile, or other categorical forms of the variable. This may be particularly relevant when scores on the measure have extreme distribution patterns. Whether or not the scores can legitimately be treated as continuous variales is one issue; specific transformations is another.

An overriding practical issue in measurement concerns relative costs associated with different approaches to data collection. These relative costs are only partially indicated in financial terms of dollars and cents; also of great importance are the human costs in terms of effort, willingness, risk, and benefit. If one were to create a hierarchy of relative research "costs" involved in different approaches to data collection in substance use research, the least costly end of the continuum might be surveys or questionnaires that participants complete independently. The most expensive end of the continuum might include some of the current biometric and physiological measurement approaches: The costs associated with equipment, devices, and technology, as well as with collecting, handling, storing, and analyzing biological samples, can frequently exceed available resources. Furthermore, as these sorts of approaches become increasingly intrusive, the associated risks also increase. The middle of the "cost" continuum might be represented by approaches that involve varying degrees of participant interaction with members of a data-collection team and varying degrees of training needed by data collectors or skilled interviewers. For example, this middle-range strategy might include telephone surveys or face-to-face interviews. The middle range might also include naturalistic observation studies with event recording by trained observers or real-time behavioral data capture (ecological momentary assessment) using diary, Smartphone, iPad, computerized time signaling, and other recording technologies (e.g., see Stone, Shiffman, Atienza, & Nebeling, 2007).

SELF-REPORT DATA

A number of scholars have accepted the challenge of analyzing the reliability and validity of self-report data, particularly data provided by individuals who have been involved with substance use (Babor, Stenberg, Anton, & Del Boca, 2000; Nyamathi, Leake, Longshore, & Gelberg, 2001; Ridley & Kordinak, 1988). These scholars generally concluded that there is good, but not perfect, concordance between what substance users report and other sources of information, such as data from biomarkers or collateral informants. These studies, however, are generally conducted with treatment-seeking individuals; we do not know how to gauge self-report accuracy in other populations and other situational circumstances. For example, Shillington and Clapp (2000) found that adolescent reports differed in their consistency depending on the substance type (alcohol use reporting was more consistent than was reporting of cigarettes and marijuana use), gender (female cigarette users were more consistent than were their male counterparts), ethnicity (cigarette and marijuana reports were more consistent for white compared to Hispanic or African American adolescents), and the measure of use (lifetime use reports were more consistent than were reports for age at onset of use). Self-reporting errors are quite possibly due to faulty recall as well as to social desirability bias or intentional falsification.

Additional complications with self-report data arise when we conduct substance use research using self-administered instruments. First, we do not know the trustworthiness of self-report data that are provided

> I tell you, addiction is a very cunning enemy.
>
> –John McCain

in unsupervised scenarios, such as knowing who actually completed a mailed or online survey, especially when incentive payments may motivate "cheating." Second, when conducting substance use research there is always the question of whether or not the self-reporting person was substance-impaired or sober when responding to the measurement tools. Self-reporting bias arising from faulty recall is potentially mitigated by ecological momentary assessment methodologies where experiences and behavior are recorded as they happen in concurrent reports, rather than recording what is recalled retrospectively (Stone et al., 2007).

One approach to improving the reliability of self-reported substance use—alcohol in particular—has received considerable attention in the research literature and has been applied in self-report studies involving other types of behaviors such as sexual risk behaviors. The Timeline Followback calendar method has been used to assess a person's drinking behavior retrospectively over the past 30 days to 1 year (Sobell & Sobell, 2000). One study applied this approach to looking at attempts at changing drinking behaviors at multiple points in a person's history as well (Begun et al., 2011). Overall, the test–retest reliability and validity assessments (content, criterion, and construct) of this approach have been favorable with measuring drinking behavior. The Timeline Followback approach can indicate patterns and variations in a person's drinking behavior as well as quantities consumed and change attempts. The approach may also be helpful in identifying specific personal drinking-related triggers. (For instructions and access to the tools, see http://www.nova.edu/gsc/online_files.html#time_followback.)

COGNITIVE IMPAIRMENT AND MEASUREMENT CHALLENGES

As always in human research, data quality is ultimately influenced by the extent to which each respondent interpreted data-collection questions and response options as intended by the researchers. But we also know from the literature concerning alcohol and other drugs that these substances can have profound short- and long-term effects on cognitive performance and human information-processing systems (Miller, 1985a). Affected are such functions as problem-solving abilities, abstract thinking, psychomotor task performance, and complex memory tasks (National Institute on Alcohol Abuse and Alcoholism, 2001). In other words, use of these substances may impair or alter how study participants respond to data-collection tools or otherwise perform during data-collection processes. Late in 2012 the National Institutes of Health (NIH) unveiled a significant resource for behavioral researchers: the NIH Toolbox for the assessment of neurological and behavioral function. This royalty-free online resource is the result of an initiative to design assessment that is minimally burdensome to subjects and investigators and to utilize "state-of-the-art" psychometric approaches and technology (e.g., computer-assisted evaluation) with the aim of improving uniformity in data compared across studies that measure human cognition, emotion, motor function, and/or sensation.

Potential Current Impairment

A major issue that researchers (and clinicians) must be prepared to address is how to handle situations when a study participant (or client receiving services) may be under the influence of alcohol or otherwise substance-impaired. First, we need to know how to identify these circumstances; then, we need to know how to manage the situation when it is encountered. In the case of concerns about alcohol impairment, many researchers screen participants at the start of each encounter (including the consent process) with a breath alcohol test as an indirect estimate of likely blood alcohol concentration (BAC measured in grams of ethanol per 100 milliliters of blood volume). A criterion point of breath alcohol–analyzed concentration equal to or greater than 0.08 (grams of ethanol per 210 liters of breath) is applied as the standard for determining that a study participant's functioning might be impaired.

Investigators who elect to administer breath alcohol tests must ensure that (1) reliable equipment is used, (2) the equipment is routinely and accurately calibrated, and (3) staff members are properly trained to use the equipment and interpret the results of the analysis. An individual's recent history of drinking may also influence the BAC levels at which impaired functioning may be inferred. You may be aware of recent legal system debates and challenges to the accuracy of data generated by "breathalyzer" analysis, and these challenges are equally relevant to research uses of the technology. A research team should be made aware of factors that can reduce the accuracy of alcohol breath analysis, such as how the person blows into the device or the time passed since consuming alcohol, as well as possibly certain medications and medical conditions. The National Highway Traffic Safety Administration Web site provides information concerning breath alcohol–detection devices that were approved (as of 2009) for screening and evidentiary use (http://www. breathalyzeralcoholtester.com/dot-approved-breathalyzer).

One practical protocol for an individual who has any detectable alcohol level on a breathalyzer involves having the person wait for 45 minutes and be retested to see if the level is rising, stable, or falling. A person who has consumed alcohol just prior to being tested may not have reached full BAC levels until the alcohol has been metabolized. The research team needs to have protocols in place for how to address this scenario as well as how to handle situations where participants "fail" this screening. The protocol should include safety plans that protect the individual and the community, such as ensuring that a person is not driving home while intoxicated, that he or she can pass through the community and/or use public transportation safely, and that the person's BAC is not reaching a level which may become a medical emergency. In general, even trained observers and practitioners will tell you that it is difficult to determine sobriety and intoxication/impairment just by looking at a person, especially persons who have a significant history of a substance use disorder and if the observer has a history of knowing that person in various states over time.

Durable Cognitive Impairment

Most of us are used to thinking about the acute, immediate effects of alcohol or other substances on a person's cognitive processes, such as knowing that drinking might impair a person's memory for events that occur during a drinking episode or a person's coordination of visual–spatial and psychomotor actions. However, we may be less aware of the potential cumulative impact of chronic drinking or substance use at risky levels, even without addiction (see National Institute on Alcohol Abuse and Alcoholism, 2001).

We also may be ill informed about cognitive impairments associated with alcohol hangover or the period of immediate recovery from abusing other substances (Prat, Adan, Pérez-Pàmies, & Sànchez-Turet, 2008). Another issue concerns the potential for cognitive impairments that might be experienced when a person who has been addicted to certain substances is undergoing detoxification, withdrawal, and early recovery, particularly when a person has experienced multiple cycles of withdrawal (Duka, Townshend, Collier, & Stephens, 2003). Even without addiction, cognitive deficits may persist for weeks after individuals stop using substances such as marijuana (Williams, 2003). On the other hand, individuals who have experienced years of cognitive impairment related to substance use or addiction may also begin to experience some recovery of abilities as sobriety periods become prolonged, as long as secondary brain diseases causing dementia remain absent (Acker, 1982).

Thus, it is imperative that researchers who collect data from individuals who have been addicted to substances consider assessing each participant's capacities for engaging effectively and accurately in the informed consent and planned data-collection processes. Some scholars have utilized the Trail Making Test, Parts A and B (Begun et al., 2011; Bowen & Harvey, 2006; Reitan, 1958) in order to assess the extent to which performance on target measures or participation in interventions might be affected by substance-induced impairments to information-processing speed, mental flexibility, and executive functioning (e.g., Begun et al., 2011; Horton & Roberts, 2003). This tool assesses at a fairly gross rather than fine level of function. Depending on the data-collection measures adopted in any particular study, it is advisable to consider including brief tools that will help determine the participants' neurocognitive capacities for engaging in the data-collection, informed consent, and participation-assent procedures at hand—memory, verbal, coordination, or other functions may need to be tapped.

CONTROLLED ENVIRONMENTS AND MEASUREMENT CHALLENGES

Substance use studies and interventions may occur in the context of controlled environments where access to alcohol and other drugs may be limited or restricted by circumstances. In some cases, clients enter treatment programs from correctional or health care facilities where their current substance use patterns were more a function of the environment rather than of their current level of functioning. In a controlled environment, the participant's quantity and frequency-of-use data may be artificially suppressed. This can pose challenges when trying to estimate the current severity of substance use disorders within a population or when conducting pre- and postcomparisons of severity. In fact, we run the risk of concluding that intervention led to a worsening of conditions if baseline data are collected under controlled environment conditions and follow-up data under more naturalistic conditions.

There is no fixed response to this issue, merely a caution to account for it when it has the potential to impact outcomes and analyses. Instead, consider using measurement tools that account for these types of circumstances, such as two widely used assessment instruments: the Addiction Severity Index (ASI; McLellan et al., 1992b) and the Global Appraisal of Individual Needs (GAIN; Dennis, White, Titus, & Unsicker, 2008). The GAIN takes the stance of determining the most recent 90-day period in which fewer than 13 days were spent in a controlled environment (Dennis et al., 2008) and then records data for that period in assessing severity. The ASI limits inquiry to the most recent 30 days regardless of the respondent's living arrangement. However, one of the interview fields instructs the interviewer to code whether or not the respondent was incarcerated during the past 30 days, allowing the researcher to take incarceration into account.

SCREENING, ASSESSMENT, AND DIAGNOSIS TOOLS

Before identifying tools that are commonly used in substance use research, it is important to think about their intended purposes. In both clinical and research practices it is important to distinguish between tools intended for screening purposes and tools intended for the purpose of assessment or diagnosis. We identify screening approaches as those designed to distinguish individuals who have or are likely to experience the target phenomenon from those who are unlikely to experience that phenomenon. Many tools are designed as brief or quick screen approaches that lead to more extensive and intensive exploration with individuals identified as being at risk for the phenomenon. We consider assessment and diagnostic tools, on the other hand, to be more extensive and intensive procedures to examine the precise nature of an individual's experience of the target phenomenon. Assessment, compared to screening, tends to be considerably more costly in time, essential staff skill sets, participant burden, and other resources. In many instances, assessment is also designed as an ongoing process, meant to be repeated periodically over time to maintain a current understanding of a person's potentially fluctuating status.

Accuracy

The first challenge that an investigator might encounter is how to accurately measure quantities of substances used by participants. The example developed in chapter 2 concerning standard drink equivalents is a useful tool to employ when the substance of interest is alcohol and when quantities can be accurately estimated. With prescription drug misuse, quantities of active ingredients may also be calculated somewhat accurately if brands and dosages are known. This quantity-assessment process becomes far more difficult when the substances involved are not regulated, such as in the case of "street," homemade, or unregulated pharmacy-produced drugs, as there is no definitive measure of active ingredients in what is actually consumed. There is also no clarity about contaminants and intentional additives.

The question of quantities consumed also becomes complicated by mode of drug administration. The amount and timing of active ingredient exposure having an effect on the body differ when substances are (1) swallowed and thereby introduced through the digestive system, (2) inhaled through smoke or vapors and introduced through the pulmonary and cardiovascular systems, (3) injected directly to the bloodstream, or (4) applied transdermally to be absorbed through the skin. Furthermore, mode of introduction is relevant to social work and public health research concerning risks of exposure to infectious diseases and probabilities of experiencing other serious health concerns.

As in the case of any screening or assessment tool, substance use disorder identification tools differ in the extent of their sensitivity and specificity: their ability to correctly identify both only and all of those individuals who actually experience the phenomenon being measured.

- *Sensitivity* of a measure refers to its being as inclusive as possible by including everyone who meets the criteria of experiencing the problem, disease, or disorder of interest. The lower an instrument's sensitivity, the greater (compared to other instruments) is the number of "false-negative" results associated with its use. In other words, increasing numbers of individuals who actually do experience the problem are classified as not having it: They are falsely classified in the "negative" category. Consider, for example, the difficulty of pregnancy testing that has poor sensitivity among substance abusing women: Too many women may believe that it is safe to drink or use because they erroneously believe they are not pregnant, only to find out later that the pregnancy test result was wrong.

- *Specificity*, on the other hand, refers to a tool's precise ability to avoid "false-positive" results. Instruments with lower specificity erroneously indicate that a person is experiencing the phenomenon being tested when, in fact, this is not true. Consider the implications of a biomarker test for fetal drug exposure that is used to determine whether or not newborn infants can go home from the hospital with their mothers. If the test has low specificity, it may overidentify drug-exposed infants, meaning that too many babies will be falsely categorized as having been prenatally exposed (compared to approaches with higher specificity).

We seek measures where, ideally, positive results happen only when the problem is really experienced (positive predictive value is good) and negative results happen only when the problem really does not exist (negative predictive value is good). Since this ideal situation is seldom encountered, social work investigators are left seeking the ideal combination of specificity and sensitivity in measurement selection, especially when counterbalanced with a need to minimize the use of more intensive, extensive, invasive, and expensive assessment strategies.

An additional accuracy issue relates to measurement stability. We can look at the extent to which applying the measurement tool results in the same conclusions being drawn time after time. For example, the Shillington and Clapp (2000) study finding discussed earlier, asking adolescents about their lifetime use of a substance, demonstrated relatively good stability: Once a student reported using that substance, each subsequent administration of the instrument tended to lead to the same positive response of having used it in his or her lifetime. However, the reported age at first use was less stably reported over time. Measurement stability becomes complicated when we attempt to measure a dynamic process, such as current use of a substance or motivation to change substance use behavior. We expect these variables to change over time, especially with intervention. Thus, we want to seek measurement tools that are also sensitive to change over time—stable when the construct being measured is actually stable, changing when the construct or behavior changes.

Screening Instrument Selection

The search for appropriate, evidence-supported screening and assessment tools can be facilitated by several resources. The first of these is the Alcohol & Drug Abuse Institute Library supported by the University of Washington (http://lib.adai.washington.edu/instruments). This library indicates the most widely used instruments having "proven reliability and validity" with a gold star, and each review includes references to articles that address specific issues in the validity and reliability of the measures as well. The National Institute on Alcohol Abuse and Alcoholism (2003) provides an overview of many instruments in their publication *Assessing Alcohol Problems: A Guide for Clinicians and Researchers*, second edition. This guide also provides a rich discussion of technique issues, such as how to approach the client/participant, providing feedback, and the importance of setting/context. In addition, the American Society of Addiction Medicine (ASAM; www.asam.org) posts recommendations and research evidence related to integrating uniform, universal screening into practice. The tools for prescreening, screening, and assessment also have utility in conducting research that requires screening. Additional resources might be considered in relation to selecting measures for screening and assessment in substance use research. The first is a review published in 1999 on assessment of alcohol and other drugs (Kazmierczak, Smyth, & Wodarski, 1999). The second is a book chapter on scales for addiction research (Darke, 2010). Investigators may also wish to consult the guide by Allen and Wilson (2003).

Table 4.1 identifies a number of potential substance use disorder screening tools that appear in the literature. We have chosen to include primarily those tools which are easily accessible to social work

Table 4.1 Behavioral Screening Instruments

Screening for	Instrument	(Re)Sources	Comments
Alcohol consumption patterns	NIAAA-recommended question sets	National Institute on Alcohol Abuse and Alcoholism (2003b)	Public domain; there are different sets of questions presented based on what information is being sought and the time to devote to the task of determining alcohol consumption patterns—3-item, 4-item, 5-item, and 6-item sets.
Alcohol involvement (adolescents)	Adolescent Alcohol Involvement Scale (AAIS)	Mayer & Filstead (1979)	Brief 14-item, self-administered measure of alcohol use (quantity) and psychosocial consequences; to identify adolescents' alcohol misuse, screen for severity of alcohol problem use
Alcohol problems	Rapid Alcohol Problems Screen	Cherpitel (2000)	Interview-administered screening for alcohol dependence during past year; 4 items for use with adults
Alcoholism	Michigan Alcoholism Screening Test (MAST)	Selzer (1971)	Public domain; these 25 items screen for lifetime alcohol-related problems and consequences; can be self- or interviewer-administered; also available in 10-item, 13-item, and 9-item brief formats; for use with adults (S-MAST is short version). There is also a version for use with geriatric populations (G-MAST)
Alcohol dependence	CAGE	Ewing (1984)	Public domain: easy-to-use four items specific to alcoholism screening where the letters C, A, G, and E stand for specific questions; for use with adults, questions arise concerning sensitivity when used with women; there is a version that is adapted to include other drugs (CAGE-IAD)
Alcohol use disorders	Alcohol Use Disorders Identification Test (AUDIT)	Babor, Higgins-Biddle, Saunders, & Monteiro (2001)	Public domain: 10 items address quantity and frequency of drinking, dependence symptoms, and problems caused by alcohol; adult measure tested with wide range of populations

(*continued*)

Table 4.1 (Continued)

Screening for	Instrument	(Re)Sources	Comments
Children of alcoholics	Children of Alcoholics Screening Test (CAST)	(test manual out of print); Sheridan (1995); Hodgins, Maticka-Tyndale, el-Guebaly, & West, (1993)	Used to determine whether or not an older child, adolescent, or adult has a parent(s) with alcohol problems; short form (CAST-6) is available
Cognitive status	Mini-Mental State Exam	Folstein, Folstein, & McHugh (1975)	Copyrighted for purchase; measures cognitive functioning in seven categories
Compulsion and craving to drink (alcohol)	Obsessive-Compulsive Drinking Scale (OCDS)	Anton, Moak, & Latham (1995)	Copyrighted and accessible on the NIAAA Web site; 14 items address drinking-related thoughts, urges to drink, and ability to resist these types of thoughts and urges; screens for alcohol abuse and dependence in adults; a version specifically for adolescents is the A-OCDS
Co-occurring disorders among those with substance abuse concerns	Global Appraisal of Individual Needs-Short Screener (GAIN-SS)	Dennis, Feeny, & Stevens (2006)	Copyrighted and requires GAIN licensure/certification credential to use; self-report screening for four areas of concern (internalizing, externalizing, substance disorders, plus crime or violence propensity)
Drug abuse or dependence disorders	Drug Abuse Screening Test (DAST; DAST-A adolescents) or Drug Use Questionnaire	Skinner (1982)	Copyrighted but free for noncommercial use; 20 items (there is a 10-item version available) for quantifying the severity of disorders related to drug use (other than alcohol); for use with adults
Drug use	Drug Use Screening Inventory-Revised	Tartar (1990); Tartar & Kirisci (1997)	Fee-for-use, self-administered screening for drug use consequences in 10 domains; 159 items; adult and adolescent versions

Nicotine dependence (cigarette smoking)	Fagerstrom Test for Nicotine Dependence	Heatherton, Kozlowski, Frecker, & Fagerstrom (1991)	Copyrighted but free for noncommercial use; six items related to cigarette smoking as indicative of quantity, dependence symptoms, and compulsion to smoke; for use with adults and adolescents who smoke cigarettes
Problem recognition (adolescents)	Problem Recognition Questionnaire	Cady, Winters, Jordan, Solberg, & Stinchfield (1996)	Adolescent self-administered quick questionnaire instrument to evaluate problem recognition and willingness to change with regard to substance use disorder
Risky drinking during pregnancy	TWEAK	Russell (1994)	Publicly available; five items designed specifically for screening women for risky drinking during pregnancy but can also be applied to adults, regardless of gender or pregnancy status; the letters stand for specific items on the inventories
Substance use/ abuse and other areas of problem functioning among adolescents	Problem Oriented Screening Instrument for Teenagers	Rahdert (1991)	Public domain; 139 items identify problem areas needing further assessment; self-administered; for use with adolescents
Substance abuse or dependence disorders	Substance Abuse Subtle Screening Inventory (SASSI)	Miller (1985b)	Copyrighted; 93 items can be self-, computer-, Web-, or support staff-administered to adults; 100 items for adolescent version (SASSI-A)
Substance involvement (includes alcohol, smoking)	Alcohol, Smoking, and Substance Involvement Screening Test (ASSIST)	WHO ASSIST Working Group (2002)	Public domain, 8 items to detect lifetime and past 3 months use of tobacco, alcohol, cannabis, cocaine, stimulants, sedatives, hallucinogens, inhalants, opioids, and other drugs; an extension of the AUDIT, NIDA provides a Web-based interactive version; for use with adults

NIAAA, National Institute on Alcohol Abuse and Alcoholism; NIDA, National Institute on Drug Abuse.

investigators and practitioners. It is important to note, however, that these screening resources and the assessment resources described below were developed and psychometrically tested during an era when the *Diagnostic and Statistical Manual of Mental Disorders*, fourth edition, Text Revision (DSM-IV-TR) criteria were applied; the field is likely to experience some transition and disruption as we begin to systematically apply and evaluate the new DSM-5 criteria and as we revalidate measurement tools in compliance with the revised diagnostic criteria. Further, the research domain criteria described by the National Institute of Mental Health (see chapter 2) may significantly alter how funding agencies view diagnostic criteria in the future. It will be important for investigators (and clinicians) to stay on top of the instrument psychometrics literature related to specific measurement protocols as we move into the new DSM-5 era.

Assessment

ASAM has had a tremendous influence on the practice of assessment and diagnosis of substance use disorders. Social work researchers engaged in research involving community-based settings are well advised to become familiar with the assessment and diagnosis protocols that are in force in these settings. Many are adopting approaches recommended by ASAM as in many cases these are the only forms of assessment for which reimbursement is made available. Working with these naturally collected data can save considerable research resources as well as eliminate the necessity of repeating assessments on individuals who are ready and primed to engage in the intervention process (Table 4.2).

Physiological and Biological Measurement Tools

Stewart, Goldmann, Neumann, and Spies (2010) suggest that the most compelling reason for addiction research to include measures of biological and physiological processes is to increase confidence in self-report and collateral sources of data. Other compelling reasons include learning about participants' physical health status vis-à-vis the substances involved as well as contributing to knowledge about the biological processes involved with substance use, addiction, and recovery. While social work researchers may place a high value on these "scientifically objective" measures, it is important to retain awareness of their limitations as

Table 4.2 Behavioral Assessment Protocols

Assessment of	Instrument	(Re)Sources	Comments
Addiction severity and global functioning	Addiction Severity Index (ASI)	McLellan et al. (1992)	In its fifth edition (since 1980); 200 items address functioning on seven subscales; can be self-administered, administered through clinical interview, or computer-administered; used with a wide array of adult populations; there is a "lite" version (ASI-lite); different versions are available for females, for baseline and follow-up, as well as for gambling (ASI-G)
Alcohol use patterns	Alcohol Timeline Followback	Sobell, Maisto, Sobell, & Cooper (1979)	Calendar-based interview protocol for assessing extent (quantity and frequency) of drinking, variability in drinking patterns, start and stop dates, time to relapse, percent days drinking or abstinent, and other variables that can be calculated from the timeline; for use with adults or adolescents. Approach has been adapted by others for use with behaviors other than drinking
Contexts of drinking behavior	Drinking Context Scale	O'Hare (2001)	23-item self-report of circumstances related to excessive drinking (three factors) for adults and adolescents
Contexts of drug use, high-risk situations	Inventory of Drug-Taking Situations	Annis, Turner, & Sklar (1997)	Self-administered, 50 items rating frequency of substance use in different situations over past year, repeated for each type of substance used; designed for adults; eight-item short form exists
Craving (alcohol)	Penn Alcohol Craving Scale	Flannery, Volpicelli, & Pettinati (1999)	Five-item self-report questionnaire about craving experiences for previous week
Expectancies about reinforcement attributes of alcohol use	Alcohol Expectancy Questionnaire (AEQ)	Brown, Christianson, & Goldman (1987)	120 statements that fit six factors associated with possible reinforcing aspects of drinking alcohol; self-administered for adults or adolescents (AEQ-A)
Family history (of alcohol problems)	Family Tree Questionnaire	Mann, Sobell, Sobell, & Sobell (1985)	Self-report of family history, identifying first- and second-degree relations who never drank or were either social drinkers, possibly problem drinkers, or definitely problem drinkers; for adults
Locus of control (drinking)	Drinking-Related Internal–External Locus of Control Scale	Hirsch, McCrady, & Epstein (1997)	Self-report questionnaire concerning beliefs regarding internal vs. external locus for drinking-related factors; adults

(continued)

Table 4.2 (Continued)

Assessment of	Instrument	(Re)Sources	Comments
Mental disorders including alcohol diagnoses	Composite International Diagnostic Interview–2nd version (CIDI-2) or World Mental Health CIDI (WMH-CIDI)	Robins et al. (1988)	Copyrighted but free to use by individuals who have been specifically trained by World Health Organization/WMH to use the CIDI; addresses criteria in both the DSM-IV and the ICD-10 schedules for alcohol dependence, alcohol abuse, harmful use, and withdrawal; for use with adults and adolescents, including those with co-occurring disorders
Mental disorders including substance abuse	Composite International Diagnostic Interview Substance Abuse Module (CIDI-SAM)	Cottler (2000)	Copyrighted with fee for use; expands the CIDI interview substance use section, including tobacco, alcohol, caffeine, and other drugs (stimulants, cannabinoids, cocaine, hallucinogens, inhalants, opiates and other sedatives, and club drugs); explores degree of impairment, symptom severity, and treatment seeking; for use with adults and adolescents
Mental disorders including substance abuse	Form 90	Miller & del Boca (1994)	Structured interview with intake, follow-up, telephone, quick, and collateral data collection; complex, requires specific training for proper administration; for adults and adolescents
Motivation, readiness to change	Readiness to Change Questionnaire (RTCQ), Treatment Version (RTCQ-TV)	Rollnick, Heather, Gold, & Hall (1992); Heather, Luce, Peck, Dunbar, & James (1999)	Self-administered brief instrument for assigning non-treatment-seeking drinkers to specific stages of the readiness cycle (treatment version for treatment seekers)
Motivation, readiness to change	Stages of Change Readiness and Treatment Eagerness Scale	Miller & Tonigan (1996)	Version 8, 19-item instrument designed to assess alcohol abusers' ambivalence, recognition, and taking steps in readiness for change; for research, not clinical use

Construct	Measure	Reference	Description
Motivation, readiness to change	University of Rhode Island Change Assessment	DiClemente & Hughes (1990)	Multiple forms exist (alcohol, drug, reduced drinking) to address motivation to change; note caution regarding use in longitudinal research designs
Problems resulting from drinking alcohol	Drinker Inventory of Consequences	Miller, Tonigan, & Longabaugh (1995)	Not copyrighted; 50-item measure of negative consequences of problematic drinking; consequences represent five domains; self-administered, for use with adults; a shorter 15-item version exists (Short Index of Problems)
Self-efficacy for abstinence (alcohol)	Alcohol Abstinence Self-Efficacy Scale	DiClemente, Carbonari, Montgomery, & Hughes (1994)	Public domain; 40 items address both efficacy for abstinence and temptation to drink/relapse; self-administered; for use with adults and adolescents
Self-efficacy for abstinence (alcohol)	Drinking Refusal Self-Efficacy Questionnaire–Revised	Oei, Hasking, & Young (2005)	Assesses beliefs about ability to resist drinking in context-specific situations (six-point scale); developed for use with adults
Substance and/or alcohol disorders and other mental health problems	Mini International Neuropsychiatric Interview (MINI)	Sheehan et al. (1998)	Questions address 16 problem areas, including alcohol abuse or dependence and substance abuse or dependence; for use with adults; a version for children and adolescents has been developed (MINI-KIDS)
Substance and/or alcohol disorders and other mental health problems	Psychiatric Research Interview for Substance and Mental Disorders	Hasin et al. (1996)	Training is required for use; semistructured, clinician-administered interview that distinguishes between effects of intoxication and withdrawal, disorders caused by substance use, and primary mental health disorders (including alcohol, drug, and other psychiatric disorders); for use with adults and adolescents
Substance and/or alcohol disorders and other mental health problems	Structured Clinical Interview for the DSM–Research Version	Riskind, Beck, Berchick, Brown, & Steer (1987)	Semistructured clinical interview; research version available from Biometric Research Department of Columbia University

(continued)

Table 4.2 (Continued)

Assessment of	Instrument	(Re)Sources	Comments
Substance abuse and needs that co-occur, global functioning	Global Appraisal of Individual Needs (GAIN)	Dennis, Titus, White, Unsicker, & Hodgkins (2002)	Requires GAIN licensure/certification credential; standardized biopsychosocial assessment interview for adults or adolescents, identifies needs and service utilization related to substance abuse and concomitant problem areas
Substance abuse by adolescents	Teen Addiction Severity Index (T-ASI)	Kaminer, Bukstein, & Tartar (1991)	Semistructured interview format for 154 items, multidimensional assessment of adolescents
Substance use disorders	Substance Use Disorders Diagnostic Schedule-IV	Hoffman & Harrison (1995); Harrison & Hoffman (2001)	Based on the DSM-IV; a version particularly structured for use with incarcerated men and women (prisoners) is available
Substance use disorders and other life problems of adolescents	Adolescent Drug Abuse Diagnosis	Friedman & Utada (1989)	150-item structured interview with severity ratings in seven domains; clinician-administered interview for adolescents
Withdrawal from alcohol	Clinical Institute Withdrawal Assessment for Alcohol–Revised	Sullivan, Sykora, Schneiderman, Naranjo, & Sellers (1989) (see Reoux & Oreskovich, 2006, for instrument copy)	10-item scale quantifies the current severity of alcohol withdrawal, repeated over time to trace the progression of withdrawal process; semistructured, clinician-administered interview

DSM-IV, *Diagnostic and Statistical Manual of Mental Disorders*, fourth edition; ICD-10, *International Classification of Diseases*, tenth revision.

Facts are not science—as the dictionary is not literature.

—Martin H. Fischer

well. For example, access to neuroimaging via magnetoencephalography (MEG), electroencephalography (EEG), and functional magnetic resonance imaging (fMRI) may not be easily accessible in all communities or close to the time when a specific experience of interest occurs.

Biomarker assay tools generally have known false-positive/false-negative testing rates reported in the literature. Not only is the specific test important to consider but also consider who will perform the analyses on collected samples. The Substance Abuse and Mental Health Services Administration Web site (samhsa.gov) maintains a list of laboratories certified as meeting minimal guidelines for federal workplace drug testing as well as drug "confirmatory cutoff" concentrations for several substances that might be analyzed in federal workplaces.

In their book chapter, Stewart et al. (2010) summarize a number of biomarker assay tests for alcohol and other drug use. The details of their discussions emphasize the point that social work investigators need to become informed about the physiology behind specific biomarker assay tests if they intend to use them wisely in their studies. For example, it is important to know the time frame around which a particular assay is accurate—designing a study where the measure is administered too soon or too long after a substance has been metabolized will lead to poor study results. The time frame within which a specific substance can be accurately detected depends, in part, on the type of tissue from which it is sampled (e.g., blood, urine, hair). The time frame also varies markedly between different types of substances (e.g., opioids, cannabinoids, alcohol; see https://www.labcorpsolutions.com/images/Drugs_of_Abuse_Reference_Guide_Flyer_3166.pdf). A good review of biomarkers related to alcohol use disorders is presented in the updated advisory published by the Substance Abuse and Mental Health Services Administration (2006).

It is important to consider the participant burden and degree of invasiveness of the different measures, as well as costs associated with their use and institutional review board concerns that arise with positive test results. Furthermore, it may become important when designing studies to consider how laboratories and participants themselves might (intentionally or unintentionally) contaminate the results of biological measurement approaches. Social work researchers may wish to consider other creative sources of physical, artifact, and archival data. For example, a count of empty beer cans may be a more accurate index of what was consumed in a solitary binge episode than is a person's recall. Or reviewing with participants their past-month debit card statement for alcohol purchases might be more informative regarding quantities, frequency, and patterns than is relying solely on personal recall (Table 4.3).

SCREENING AND ASSESSMENT AS INTERVENTION

As researchers and clinicians, we generally think of screening and assessment interactions as "preintervention" events because, temporally at least, they come before we deliver or engage clients in a planned intervention approach. However, it appears that this is not the way that all participants in intervention research experience the screening and assessment processes. Epstein et al. (2005) demonstrated that female participants in at least one randomized clinical trial significantly improved their drinking patterns (decreased percent drinking days) during the period between assessment completion and beginning the intervention for an alcohol use disorder. This introduces questions for intervention research regarding the extent to which screening and assessment procedures act as interventions themselves and/or the extent to which seeking treatment (volunteering to enter an intervention study) affects behavior, even without intervention. Furthermore, it may explain why some potentially promising interventions are not associated with statistically greater improvement than control groups: Many individuals in both groups are changed by the study entry process.

The Substance Abuse and Mental Health Services Administration has also supported a number of research studies demonstrating that a process of screening, brief intervention, and referral to treatment (SBIRT) is associated with meaningful levels of change in participants studied within different settings (e.g., primary care, emergency departments). The SBIRT protocol is reasonably well developed and defined as an intervention approach, and social work investigators may be interested in looking into how it works in a more diverse range of settings, with more diverse populations, and under a broader range

Table 4.3 Biological, Physiological, Biomarker Tools

Category	Goal/Objective	Specific Examples
Imaging/ neuroimaging	To visualize anatomical structures and/ or physiological processes (brain, other organs)	• CT scan (computed tomography) • CAT scan (computerized axial tomography) • MRI scan (magnetic resonance imaging) • fMRI scan (functional MRI) • PET scan (positron emission tomography) • Brain SPECT (single photon emission computed tomography)
On-site or lab tests for substance use (direct measures)	To measure presence and/or concentration of a substance or its breakdown/residual products (metabolites) in breath, urine, blood, sweat, saliva, hair, or other tissue	• Breath analyzer • Single- or multipanel test kits • Ethyl glucuronide (EtG), ethyl sulfate, (EtS); phosphatidylethanol—(PEth) an emerging possibility
Lab tests for clinical conditions associated with substance abuse/ addiction (indirect measures)	To measure presence of disease processes that may result from substance abuse or the condition of addiction in the body	• Liver damage: gamma-glutamyl transferase (GGT), alanine amino transferase (ALT)/serum glutamic pyruvic transaminase (SGPT), aspartate amino transferase (AST)/serum glutamic-oxaloacetic transaminase (SGOT) • Red blood cells: mean corpuscular volume (MCV) • Other metabolic processes: carbohydrate-deficient transferrin (CDT) • Disease/disorder: human immunodeficiency virus (HIV), hepatitis C, tuberculosis
Environmental tobacco smoke (ETS) exposure	Indicates second-hand smoke exposure (or primary smoker)	Cotinine
Neurotransmitter levels, genomics	Possible predictors of response to treatment for substance use disorders	Norepinephrine, serotonin, phenylethylamine(PEA), gamma-aminobutyric acid (GABA)

of implementation circumstances (see www.samhsa.gov for more information related to SBIRT). For example, providing screening and feedback using a motivational interviewing approach may also make a difference in substance use outcomes among women reentering the community following a period of incarceration (Begun et al., 2009). Bliss and Pecukonis (2009) have outlined a substance use disorder screening and brief intervention practice model for social workers in practice settings where substance use disorders may be encountered despite this not being their primary mission to address. In short, it is important for social work researchers to consider the power of these processes for altering behavior outside of the intervention context. This is relevant as a confound in designing or interpreting any substance use intervention research study as well as in making these processes a specific focus of intervention research efforts.

MEASUREMENT BEYOND THE INDIVIDUAL LEVEL

Social work investigators may wish to study substance-related topics that address interactions between individuals' behaviors and the social contexts in which they function—family, groups, neighborhoods, organizations, and other of the larger social system contexts important in ecological theory (Bronfenbrenner, 2005). Or they may be interested in interactions between individuals and these larger system elements. If studies are properly designed and multilevel measurement is conducted, investigators have hierarchical linear modeling analysis as a tool for examining person–environment factors related to substance use. In their study of party characteristics (as environmental contexts) and individual characteristics related to alcohol consumption patterns, Clapp, Min, Shillington, Reed, and Croff (2008) applied this systems approach. Measurement included both individual behavioral measures (including a brief questionnaire and breathalyzer results to estimate blood alcohol levels) and contextual measures (e.g., time of night the party occurred, size of the party, and whether or not the party had a theme). Similarly, Clapp et al. (2009) studied the impact of bar environments on individual-level drinking through a combination of individual- and contextual-level measurement approaches, demonstrating that factors at both levels contribute to variation in bar patrons' blood alcohol levels.

MEASURING INTERVENTION PROCESS ELEMENTS

Substance use disorders intervention research is not always just about outcomes. In many instances, social work investigators address questions concerning intervention processes and the features of behavioral interventions that account for the observed outcomes. The aim of this sort of investigation is to open the "black box of treatment" that exists between "inputs" of the client system experiencing problems with substance use and "outputs" or intervention outcomes (see Longabaugh et al., 2005).

Measures such as days of program participation and discharge status represent two fairly simplistic types of process variable. Measuring the types and amount of services provided through a program also can be important, more complex variables for both organization- and individual-level analyses. The Treatment Services Review (TSR; McLellan, Alterman, Cacciola, Metzger, & O'Brien, 1992a) shows us how to measure the range of services provided during a treatment experience. This brief instrument is designed for weekly administration during the treatment process, typically taking only a few minutes to complete. The TSR assesses treatment services in seven domains, compatible with the assessment domains of the ASI (McLellan et al., 1992a). Combining the two measures (TSR and ASI) allows for an assessment of the match between client need, as measured by addiction severity, and the provision of treatment services. There is also a version for adolescents (Kaminer, Blitz, Burleson, & Sussman, 1998).

The Longabaugh et al. (2005) review article identifies several lines of study indicating "active ingredients" that may be candidates for explaining the effects of various types of interventions in alcohol and other substance use disorder studies. The study of mediating factors requires specific research design strategies but also may necessitate the development and evaluation of new measurement tools. For example, as attention turns to the role of therapeutic alliance in substance use treatment outcomes, investigators will need valid and reliable approaches for qualitatively and quantitatively assessing therapeutic alliance in the types of settings and with the types of clients engaged in substance use intervention research (see Elvins & Green, 2008). Social work investigators may also wish to collaborate with scientists engaged in neurobiological study since many of the change processes stimulated through behavioral intervention are operationalized through brain–behavior mechanisms.

Another key process measurement issue for social work investigators to consider is the extent to which a substance use disorder intervention approach is characterized as being both developmentally and culturally competent for the individuals involved (see Straussner, 2001).

But how should this complex mediator be measured systematically, given that competencies differ by specific cultural, ethnic, gender, sexual orientation, spiritual, and other context dimensions (see Stanhope, Solomon, Pernell-Arnold, Sands, & Bourjoll, 2005)? For the most part, the literature examines the cultural competence of individual practitioners, leaving us with little in the way of tools for assessing the competency aspect of interventions and intervention protocols. While we do not offer recommendations of specific measurement tools for the many different substance use intervention processes and mediators, we do strongly recommend that social work investigators devote effort to their identification and/ or development when proceeding with plans to conduct substance use disorder intervention studies.

MEASURING INTERVENTION FIDELITY AND INTEGRITY

A critical measurement and analysis feature of substance use intervention research is the way in which fidelity to the intervention protocol is managed, monitored, and evaluated—in other words, the integrity of the intervention delivery process. Glasgow (2009) refers to poor and poorly documented intervention fidelity as a source of Type III error in intervention research studies. As noted by Carroll et al. (2000), while the adaptability of behavioral interventions is an essential strength, their dynamic nature also terrifically complicates study efforts. These authors provide substance use researchers with an option for evaluating intervention fidelity as distinct from measuring interventionist competence in comparing three addiction treatment approaches: clinical management of medication (also called "compliance management"), 12-step facilitation (TSF), and cognitive-behavioral therapy (CBT). Particularly helpful in this article about the Yale Adherence and Competence Scale is the authors' description of their process in developing a systematic fidelity assessment strategy. Another fidelity example in the substance use arena is presented by Chawla et al. (2010) as a means of assessing the integrity of intervention delivery in a mindfulness-based relapse prevention study: the Mindfulness-Based Relapse Prevention Adherence and Competence Scale.

Articles concerning fidelity clearly address the extent to which investigators manualized the intervention approach, trained the interventionists, and monitored the integrity of delivery (Bond, Drake, McHugo, Rapp, & Whitley, 2009; Naleppa & Cagle, 2010; Tucker & Blythe, 2008). The other side of intervention fidelity, however, involves the extent to which it was received as intended. Substance use researchers need to consider measuring the extent to which intervention recipients understood what is being presented to them or asked of them as well as evaluating the recipients' ability to implement the new skills and knowledge in their own real-world contexts (see Borelli, 2011).

ORGANIZATION-LEVEL MEASUREMENT

Evidence indicates a number of organizational factors that may contribute to program performance and client outcomes. Many differences in client outcomes appear to occur independently of the treatment modality (D'Aunno, 2006), and studies have associated differential client satisfaction, engagement, and outcomes with specific organizational characteristics, such as program size and staffing patterns (D'Aunno, 2006), turnover (Knight, Becan, & Flynn, 2012), and organizational climate or culture (Broome, Flynn, Knight, & Simpson, 2007; Melnick, Wexler, Chaple, & Banks, 2006). Failing to take into account organizational characteristics in multisite studies can confound results (Melnick et al., 2006). The implementation and retention of empirically based treatment approaches appear to vary as a function of organizational characteristics as well (Roman & Johnson, 2002). These findings represent a very rich opportunity for organizational research in the addictions.

To that point, D'Aunno (2006) called for an increase in organizational research within the substance use arena. This call for action addressed both the organizational level, which includes variables such as the size, mission, and funding characteristics of organizations as well as studying staff as individuals and as groups. Staff-level research tends to consider turnover, motivation, and training. D'Aunno (2006) noted that, while we know a great deal about treatment outcomes, we know less about the impact of organizational process on intervention outcomes; and there is much to be learned by studying the interaction of these two levels as a source of influence on outcomes.

Variables that one might include in an organizational analysis often can be measured directly. This includes variables such as caseload size, staff credentials, and payor mix, to name just a few. Here the usual measurement cautions apply in terms of carefully defining variables and ensuring the accuracy with which administrative information systems record data. One source of instruments for collecting this sort of data is the National Drug Abuse Treatment System Survey, a multiwave study consisting of both program administrator and clinician surveys (D'Aunno & Price, 2009). These surveys facilitated data collection on a number of organization-level factors, including referral sources, staffing, funding, and interprogram collaboration. The National Drug Abuse Treatment System Survey also includes a section focused on documenting recent changes in programming. The survey team has done the work of defining many of the terms, the surveys are available online, and these might easily be adapted to solicit program- and organization-level data for future studies.

In addition to many direct measures, there are important organizational constructs associated with program performance. A number of scholars have offered measures to assess constructs such as organizational culture and climate, staff satisfaction, staff and client engagement, and organizational readiness to change. For example, Van Saane, Sluiter, Verbeek, and Fings-Dresen (2003) conducted a systematic review of staff satisfaction measures employed in health care settings. McMurtry and Hudson (2000) presented a 25-item inventory for assessing consumer satisfaction that may be of interest, one that is available in a Spanish version as well (McMurtry & Torres, 2002). Other sources of organizational measures can be found in the Jung et al. (2009) review of 48 instruments designed to measure organizational culture.

Additionally, the Institute of Behavioral Research at Texas Christian University (http://www.ibr.tcu.edu/index.htm) has presented a great deal of research in the area of organizational change in the substance use arena and has developed a set of widely used measures. Simpson (2002) provides a useful conceptual model for organizational change to support the development of research questions in this area. Lehman, Greener, and Simpson (2002) described an instrument for assessing organizational readiness to change. Their 115-item survey assesses a range of organizational characteristics and has the potential for wide application in conducting organizational research. The survey includes 18 different scales organized in four areas: motivational readiness, institutional resources, staff attributes, and organizational climate. The Survey of Organizational Functioning (Broome et al., 2007) incorporates the Organizational Readiness to Change survey along with another nine scales that include measures of staff satisfaction and burnout.

In a similar vein, Rubin and Parrish (2011) present investigators with the Evidence-Based Practice Process Assessment Scale for determining practitioners' knowledge, attitudes, and practice behaviors with regard to employing an evidence-based practice process. Ager et al. (2011) also developed an instrument to measure these dimensions (knowledge, attitudes, and behaviors) with regard to a specific type of substance use intervention: motivational enhancement therapy (MET). Their novel instrument, created out of a detailed literature review, also measured practitioners' diffusion networks, change agent exposure, and organizational characteristics related to the motivational enhancement therapy (MET) approach.

COMMUNITY-LEVEL MEASUREMENT

There are many opportunities to answer important research questions with community-level measures, by collecting and aggregating individual-level data or by analyzing existing data on community conditions and characteristics. Examples of community-level studies might include assessing the impact of community prevention efforts, the consequences of policy changes, or the impact of law enforcement practices or describing community-level conditions and treatment needs. An important arena for social work investigation related to substance use involves service and delivery system access, utilization, and barriers. Investigators may find community-level data through the service delivery systems that they are interested in studying. For example, Ryan, Marsh, Testa, and Louderman (2006) were able to address important social work research questions through child welfare services data sources.

When contemplating work with community-level data, it is worth restating the caution of the ecological fallacy (Robinson, 1950). Variable relationships that exist at the community level may not be present at the individual level or may even occur in a different direction. One may not make inferences about individual characteristics based on what is observed at the community level. For example, one may find that communities with high rates of single-parent households and unemployment have higher rates of treatment need. That finding cannot be interpreted as empirical support for a finding that unemployed single parents are a greater risk for substance use or substance use disorders. Similarly, as data are aggregated to a higher level, for example, aggregating individual survey responses to create a community-level indicator, relationships between the variables can change and should be viewed with caution. In a related critique Schwartz (1994) described the flaw of assigning group-level characteristics to all members of the group as a construct validity problem.

The Communities That Care study is an example of aggregating data collected at the community level to assess community function (Hawkins & Catalano, 2002). To test a community-level intervention, the Communities That Care surveys primarily secondary school–aged children regarding such behaviors as substance use and delinquent or violent behavior, along with a number of both individual and community characteristics. Data are aggregated to determine the presence of risk and protective factors at the community level and to make comparisons between intervention communities and matched comparison communities.

While individual surveys are a common approach to assessing community function, there are often significant impediments to doing so. Measuring community function through surveys is expensive, even at the local level. While using secondary data sources such as the National Survey on Drug Use and Health (NSDUH) can be an option, it is often the case that appraisals are desired at substate levels, for which insufficient data are collected to make accurate estimates.

Additionally, adopting an environmental perspective may require measures of conditions that are not best obtained through individual surveys. Variables such as liquor supplier density (Livingston, Chikritzhs, & Room, 2007; Campbell et al., 2007), alcohol tax receipts and consumption (Purshouse, Meier, Brennan, Taylor, & Rachid, 2010; Norström, 2004), poverty and unemployment (Mossakowski, 2008), the percentage of renter-occupied property (Sanchez, Dunteman, Kuo, Yu, & Bray, 2001), high school dropout rates (Barton, Watkins, & Jarjoura, 1997), fatality rates (Giacopassi & Winn, 1995), and certain crime rates (Liu, Siegel,

& Brewer, 1997; Garriott, 1993; Harrison & Gfroerer, 1992) are among those that have been shown to be correlated with, if not causally related to, the level of problem severity and substance use disorder treatment need. Social norms, such as those prevalent on a college campus, represent another potentially important set of "community"-level variables.

In addition to being well suited for the study of community-level conditions, community or social indicator approaches offer other potential benefits. Their use offers the possibility of developing estimates at any regional level for which indicator data are available. This approach can be used to compare geographic areas, particularly at the substate level (Simeone, Frank, & Aryan, 1993). Social or community indicator approaches can be implemented at a relatively low cost, particularly when compared to household-level surveys. As a result, it becomes feasible to replicate such a study on a regular basis to update findings and identify trends over time. Social indicator data are commonly used to update estimates developed from less frequently implemented household surveys (Gregoire, Burke, Moon, Ginzer, & Joliff, 2006; Gregoire, 2002).

There are a number of public sources of social indicator data. Many can now be downloaded directly from state agency Web sites. State health departments can provide data on vital statistics that may be correlated with substance use including substance-related deaths, low–birth weight deliveries, and adult deaths due to health conditions such as HIV/AIDs, hepatitis C, or liver disease. Data available from criminal justice or correctional systems also may include substance-related indicators such as drug or alcohol-related arrests, intimate partner violence, and other violent crimes. Graduation and school dropout data are often available from state boards of education. Economic development agencies may provide data on alcohol sales, the number of liquor licenses in a given area, and employment statistics. These data often can be provided at the county level if the services are provided on a county basis.

The US Census Bureau is another commonly used source of indicator data. American Fact Finder, a tool on the bureau's Web site (http://factfinder2.census.gov/), allows the downloading of data collected from the decennial census, as well as annual estimates made for a number of population conditions, including age, race and ethnicity, sex, poverty, and employment. Data can be downloaded at a number of levels: national, statewide, and census tract. The Area Resource File (http://arf.hrsa.gov/) is a database maintained by the US Department of Health and Human Services Health Resources and Services Administration. The Area Resource File contains county-level data collected from a variety of sources including the US Census Bureau, the Bureau of Labor Statistics, the National Center for Health Statistics, and the Centers for Medicare and Medicaid Services. The Area Resource File is a great source for county-level data on numerous variables of potential interest to substance use researchers, including expenditures, income, employment, housing status, population density, and hospital utilization.

The Health Resources and Services Administration gathers and disseminates statistics related to the health services needed and utilized by Americans who are uninsured or "medically vulnerable" (see www.hrsa.gov/index.html). It is a rich resource for substance use investigators interested in human services research, particularly with reference to women's health, maternal–child outcomes, child and adolescent health, and mental health care.

When comparing different geographical areas, particularly across state boundaries, it is important to become familiar with the data so as to be certain that they are being defined and measured in the same way in each locale. For example, state differences in the definition of legal levels of intoxication result in different rates of arrest that are a function of the problem definition rather than a proxy for problem severity. It can also be challenging to determine the meaning of some indicator data, particularly in the case of enforcement data. For example, does an increase in arrests for drug possession or impaired driving signal an increase in the incidence of the problem or a change in enforcement practices?

The same guidelines apply when merging data from different public sources. Findings based on a higher level of analysis, for example, the state level, may not inform important questions about regional, county, or census tract levels. When possible, it is desirable to have collected disaggregated community-level data: data specific for smaller geographic areas (i.e., counties rather than states) or subsets of the population based on age, sex, race/ethnicity, or other relevant demographics. Merging indicator data from different sources may pose problems when derived from different political levels, such as counties versus school districts. Data-collection periods may also vary between social indicator sources, with some data being collected on a 12-month calendar cycle and other data collected on a fiscal year or other time frame. Combining data collected during different time periods has the potential to introduce spurious relationships due to the time lag and data relationships that are a function of changes in policy or practices and resulting from significant events during a specific time period.

CHAPTER CONCLUSIONS

The level at which data are measured is an important consideration— from the biological/physiological systems within individuals to the macro-systems within which individuals, families, groups, organizations, institutions, and cultural systems function. A wide array of tools may be available to social work investigators for reliably measuring substance-related constructs. A considerable number and range of practical issues, however, go into determining the measurement approaches best suited to any particular study: specificity and sensitivity, degree of invasiveness, appropriateness to the populations involved as participants, and others. Different measurement strategies apply to the nature of the study variables as well: indicators of behavior, intervention process, intervention fidelity, and context variables appear on the list. Fortunately, there exists a wealth of resources for investigators to consult in designing their measurement strategies.

5

Studying Dissemination and Implementation of Substance Use Research

While it is certainly necessary, it is not sufficient for substance use science simply to test the efficacy and effectiveness of preventive and treatment interventions. It is at least as important for the field to identify, develop, and empirically evaluate strategies, methods, and systems for research-tested interventions to be implemented in practice and policy settings (National Institutes of Health, 1999). A number of scholars have noted the extreme length of the average time lag between when empirical evidence becomes available and when it becomes integrated into routine practice: It takes as much as 17 to 20 years for only about 14% of such knowledge to become part of routine health care practice (Colditz, 2012; Westfall, Mold, & Fagnan, 2007). There exist a number of barriers to moving empirical evidence into routine practice and witnessing the potential benefits across the population (Sung et al., 2003), and there is no particular reason to believe that the picture is any rosier with regard to behavioral health science and practice.

Integral to the translational science framework introduced in chapter 1 is the body of research that addresses how our best evidence-informed substance use knowledge comes to inform practice or fails to do so. We need to understand the factors and processes by which evidence-informed practices in substance use science become adopted and implemented by practitioners, programs, organizations, institutions, policy decision makers, and client/consumer audiences. These issues and principles appear to be transdisciplinary, spanning medical and behavioral sciences; the social work, nursing, psychology, education, medicine, business, and allied health professions; and research domains that include substance use and addictions (see Brownson, Colditz, & Proctor, 2012).

The National Institutes of Health (NIH) have committed significant resources to research that helps "identify, develop, and refine effective and efficient methods, structures, and strategies to disseminate and implement" interventions that have been research-tested into public health and clinical practice settings (see http://grants.nih.gov/grants/guide/pa-files/PAR-10-038.html#PartII). In essence, this area of investigation is concerned with promoting the integration of scientific knowledge and evidence-informed approaches into routine practice. Substance use investigators are faced with the challenge of studying mechanisms for translating evidence-based knowledge and evidence-informed intervention into elements that will be useful and utilized by consumers, care providers, and program planners, as well as informing policy at the local, state, national, and global levels.

DISSEMINATION IN THE FIELD OF SUBSTANCE USE

Dissemination activities are intentional and lead to innovative information or technology being distributed to specific audiences. The intent with dissemination is to spread these innovations as broadly and deeply into that audience as possible. Dissemination is contrasted with *diffusion* in terms of their relative activity and intentionality: diffusion is a far more passive process of information or technology dispersal (see Rogers, 1995a). Interesting to consider are parallels between how an epidemiologist might study the diffusion of a new drug-involved behavior (e.g., the appearance of a new drug on the scene or a new mode of administering

> Research can be a big clunker.
>
> –Michael Ondaatje

drugs) and how we might study diffusion (or lack thereof) for new treatment or intervention strategies. New and emerging methodologies for studying social networks and system complexity, as well as social media movements and technologies, offer exciting research opportunities in this area.

Dissemination also is contrasted with *implementation*, which involves utilization of the disseminated innovation by the target audience or its integration into routine practice and in specific settings. Simpson (2002) argues that in the field of substance use disorders treatment, far more is understood about dissemination than about the rest of the technology transfer process. Dissemination of research findings clearly becomes only a part of the implementation formula: Infusion of research findings into practices and policies involves a far more complex set of processes. Dissemination and implementation together comprise a set of processes by which we see practices with an evidence base become adopted or "infused" into practice. Other terms that have been used interchangeably or in an overlapping manner include knowledge utilization and technology transfer (see Dearing, 2008; Rabin & Brownson, 2012; and a review by the RUSH Project, http://www.researchutilization.org/matrix/resources/review/).

According to innovation adoption theories, whether or not a particular evidence-based intervention is ever or routinely delivered by practitioners depends on a number of factors (Stelk, 2006). Some of the factors to consider in research about these processes include whether or not practitioners know about an innovative intervention, "adopter" characteristics of the practitioners exposed to the innovation, how well the intervention is actually suited to their client/client system circumstances (i.e., it is palatable), costs associated with delivery of the intervention, agency and reimbursement policies, availability of alternative interventions (evidence-based or not), complexity of the innovative intervention, adoption outcomes that are detectable or palpable by practitioners, and whether or not practitioners have developed competency in its delivery (Dearing, 2008; Fraser et al., 2009; Green, Ottoson, Garcia, & Hiatt, 2009; Stelk, 2006). This branch of science is also concerned with assessing the fidelity with which an intervention is implemented, how local entities modify it in their real-world circumstances, assessing impact at the adoption sites, and means of enhancing the adoption readiness of client systems, practitioners, organizations, communities, or policy decision makers.

While dissemination is a key step in moving scientific knowledge into practice, it is not necessarily the best first step. Dissemination involves a set of processes facilitated by the involvement of key stakeholders in the earliest phases of research development and execution: Research that is informed by practice leads to intervention programs that are suited to the populations and settings where they are intended to be applied (Fraser et al., 2009). In chapter 2 we introduced the issue of their inclusion early in a study's development and throughout its implementation; here, we add the importance of their involvement in making and evaluating any localized or tailored adaptations that render adoption more comfortable and sustainable. Early involvement of potential users in the planning, development, and research concerning an innovative psychosocial or behavioral intervention is a condition with demonstrated influence on the intervention's ultimate adoption (Backer, Liberman, & Kuehnel, 1986).

Much of the research in this area is built on a foundation concerning the diffusion and dissemination of innovations pioneered by Rogers (e.g., 1995b). Another major influence is the body of work building on principles and measures of organizational readiness to change its practices or readiness to adopt novel approaches (e.g., Backer, 1995; Simpson, 2002). Simpson (2002) suggests that perceived need and pressure for change define the motivation of program leaders and staff members to adopt new approaches or technologies. The types of dissemination research in which social work investigators might engage include, but are not limited to, the following:

- exploring the circumstances under which substance use research evidence is spread through a community of practitioners, within agencies, and between organizations
- identifying factors that determine the extent to which both transmission and reception of empirical substance use–related information occurs

- developing an understanding of how these processes or factors compare between audiences such as consumers, care providers, program administrators, professional educators, and policy decision makers (see http://grants.nih.gov/grants/guide/pa-files/PAR-10-038.html#PartII)

Simpson (2002) was part of the team at Texas Christian University that developed a series of tools for assessing organizational readiness to change and the impact of workshop training sessions. Among these are the Organizational Readiness for Change (TCU ORC) assessment, the Program Training Needs (TCU PTN) survey, the Workshop Evaluation,(TCU WEVAL) and the Workshop Assessment at Follow-Up(TCU WAFU).

As part of its mission, the Addiction Technology Transfer Center (ATTC) network, funded by the Center for Substance Abuse Treatment (CSAT), has engaged in dissemination activities, raising awareness of promising and best-practice approaches to intervention around substance use and addiction (see http://www.attcnetwork.org). The concept of "technology" in this sense is not just about computer hardware and software but reflects all of the tools and interventions applied in the substance use and addiction domain. The network's emphasis is on the dissemination of evidence-based practices that are either prevention- or treatment-oriented (see e.g., Sorensen, Lin, & Sera, 2004). The Addiction Technology Transfer Centers were also charged with promoting changes that lead to improved treatment services in the addictions.

Social work (and other professional) education represents a recognized mechanism for potentially disseminating the evidence base related to substance use and addiction practices. A number of studies published over the years have examined preservice or in-service education for preparing social work professionals to address substance use and addiction. The research concerning education as a dissemination approach indicates that, while social workers often play key roles in providing substance-related services to individuals, families, communities, and organizations affected by substance use problems, they may be underprepared by their

---

The saddest aspect of life right now is that science gathers knowledge faster than society gathers wisdom.

–Isaac Asimov

training to do so effectively (Amodeo & Fassler, 2000; Amodeo et al., 2002; Berger, Otto-Salaj, Stoffel, Hernandez-Meier, & Gromoske, 2009; Bina et al., 2008; Decker, Brenner, & Murtagh, 2005; Gassman, Demone, & Albilal, 2001; Hall, Amodeo, Shaffer, & VanderBilt, 2000; Lemieux & Schroeder, 2004; Quinn, 2010; Richardson, 2007, 2008; Senreich & Straussner, 2013; Straussner & Vairo, 2007; Sun, 2001). Perceived difficulty in learning an evidence-supported practice is a predictor of service providers' lower knowledge, skills, and self-efficacy for applying it (Ager et al., 2011). Recruiting and training substance use treatment program supervisors may prove to be an effective, albeit difficult, means of facilitating greater adoption by practitioners of evidence-supported intervention approaches (Amodeo, Storti, & Larson, 2010; Straussner et al., 2006).

Finally, we come full circle with chapter 1 where we examined the sources to which scholars might turn for empirical literature concerning substance use and addiction. We also turn to these same sources as potential outlets for disseminating our research findings. A tool that social work investigators may wish to consult in preparing for dissemination of their efforts is *Publishing Addiction Science: A Guide for the Perplexed*, second edition, by Babor, Stenius, Savva, & O'Reilly (2008). There is also a related Web site called PARINT (Publishing Addiction Research Internationally) that provides guidance in the dissemination of research results across national and language borders (http://www.parint.org). Related to the content below concerning implementation science, there is a specific dissemination vehicle to consider as well: the journal *Implementation Science*.

DISSEMINATION RESEARCH AS INTERVENTION RESEARCH

In terms of research design, dissemination efforts can be treated as any other sort of intervention where the intervention (X) is designed to promote dissemination of an evidence-informed innovation in substance use treatment

> You can do the best research and be making the strongest intellectual argument, but if readers don't get past the third paragraph you've wasted your energy and valuable ink.
>
> —Carl Hiaasen

practice or policy (see chapter 2 on research design strategies). For example, dissemination strategies might be studied through randomized and other controlled experimental comparisons, as well as time series and pre-/post-/ follow-up designs. While recognizing similarities in some of the design, measurement, and methodological approaches, it is critical to maintain an appreciation for the distinction between research that extends the profession's knowledge base to inform substance use interventions and research that informs how to implement interventions (Proctor & Rosen, 2008).

One option discussed by Landsvark et al. (2012) is the "roll-out" design approach. In this type of implementation study the investigators first divide all of the available study units (programs or communities) into comparable sets, similar to a matched-pair design approach. Prior to initiating the effort to elicit adoption or implementation of the innovation, investigators begin by measuring the target implementation outcome variables: Data are collected from all of the entities (programs or communities) engaged in the study. Random assignment within each comparable set occurs next, with the randomization reflecting when implementation will be initiated with each entity. The roll-out concept applies here because all of the entities will eventually be exposed to the implementation condition. In this manner, each entity still serves as its own control over time and the entities can be compared by their exposure status at different times.

Herie and Martin (2002) discuss knowledge diffusion, dissemination, technology transfer, and social marketing of addiction treatment modalities for social work. The authors present a five-step model for incorporating theory into dissemination research:

- assessing needs, gaps, and opportunities for dissemination and potential adoption of the innovation
- identifying and engaging target systems for a dissemination-oriented intervention
- field testing the dissemination intervention strategy
- disseminating more broadly
- gathering feedback data and providing ongoing consultation to adopters of the innovation

The Herie and Martin (2002) framework, however, is perhaps too unidirectional in nature: It primarily addresses how innovations can be pushed out into the practice arena. Other scholars emphasize the bidirectional complement: preparedness for receiving and infusing an innovation into practice. Specifically, substance use practitioners, programs, and treatment systems need to be both willing and able to adopt an innovation. In other words, they need to be ready for change (Weiner et al., 2008).

Of further significance are characteristics and qualities of the innovations themselves that warrant attention by investigators interested in adoption and dissemination processes. For example, Miller and Manuel (2008) studied the size-of-effect thresholds for clinically meaningful differences that practitioners view as justification for learning to employ a new treatment method. They found that this effect size threshold differs depending on the nature of the outcome being evaluated. When patient mortality is the outcome of concern, five percentage points difference between the innovation and standard practice was a relevant adoption point; for other dichotomous outcomes, differences of 10–12 percentage points for numbers who improved with the innovation were necessary. When outcomes were reflected in continuous variable measurements, the "tipping point" for practitioner adoption was double the base rate for a positive outcome or half the base rate for a negative outcome.

READINESS TO ADOPT INNOVATIONS

The research literature links a number of organizational factors with the extent to which evidence-based practices become integrated into routine practice. Roman and Johnson (2002) identified organizational characteristics associated with the extent to which treatment with the medication naltrexone became infused in substance use treatment efforts, concluding that payment schedules and patient relapse patterns witnessed by the organization were important features. Another essential factor for the adoption of substance use intervention practices with empirical evidence behind them may involve whether or not organizations are primarily substance use treatment agencies or have other primary missions and goals but encounter substance use–related service needs among those they serve (Patterson & McKiernan, 2010). This becomes relevant to the substance use research adoption and implementation processes along a number of dimensions, including whether or not the programs operate within the dissemination stream, the culture and climate of the organizations with regard to substance use intervention practices, and resources for adoption, including the extent to which staff are prepared with the requisite knowledge, skills, and beliefs for adoption of the innovations.

Approaches for the measurement of organizational readiness to change or to adopt an innovation are important contributions to the development of implementation research in substance use and addiction. Weiner et al. (2008) present a review of literature concerning how this construct has been conceptualized and operationalized in 43 different measurement tools. The authors conclude that only a fraction of the tools reported in health research are presented with adequate psychometric validation. In the end, they identify only a handful of instruments that had undergone what they considered to be adequate, systematic validity and reliability assessment.

Among the pool of valid and reliable tools to consider is the relatively popular Texas Christian University ORC instrument. The TCU ORC originally developed out of the substance use and addiction field and addresses readiness at both the programmatic and individual practitioner levels (Lehman et al., 2002). The tool's authors caution, however, that interrater reliability coefficients across studies have not consistently fallen into the acceptable range.

Another approach to measuring organizational readiness to change is offered by Holt, Armenakis, Field, and Harris (2007). This measure is specific to a proposed change and is designed for the individual level of analysis rather than the organizational level. Janson (2004) and Herscovitch and Meyer (2002) offer measures with a slightly different emphasis: the commitment to change professional practices among an organization's membership.

Publication of the Brief Individual Readiness for Change Scale (BIRCS; Goldman, 2009) is more recent than the Weiner et al. (2008) review. It is intended specifically for use with practitioners in substance treatment programs to assess individual practitioners' readiness to change and is derived, in part, from the ORC mentioned above (Goldman, 2009; Lehman et al., 2002). The instrument asks about using direct service techniques based on research, not about any specific research-informed approach. The scale's authors suggest treating the tool like a staff member–screening instrument, prior to entering into the use of lengthier, more costly assessment strategies.

SUBSTANCE USE COST–EFFECTIVENESS RESEARCH

Substance use researchers may wish to develop cost–effectiveness components in association with their intervention outcome studies. Since the 1970s, cost–effectiveness research has emerged as a way of contributing to program and policy decision making and may even be viewed as an ethical responsibility for intervention researchers, especially when study aims include comparative effectiveness analysis (Sidora-Arcoleo & Frick, 2012). The primary purpose behind cost–effectiveness studies is, in essence, to determine the amount of benefit conferred in relation to the cost of delivering the intervention protocol. While efficacy and comparative effectiveness studies can demonstrate and compare outcomes and side effects, cost–effectiveness research can tell us which among a set of efficacious approaches have cost-to-benefit ratios that are acceptable for their adoption on a wider scale.

A first step in the process is to identify the outcomes to be evaluated (Royse, Thyer, Padgett, & Logan, 2001). The Centers for Disease Control and Prevention training module on cost–effectiveness analysis suggests selecting outcomes such as "number of cases prevented" with an intervention approach or "years of life saved" through intervention (see entire interactive learning module at http://www.cdc.gov/owcd/EET/CostEffect2/fixed/1.html). Substance use investigators might select any of a number of outcome variables presented in chapter 2 for meeting this research aim.

A next step involves identifying and quantifying the costs and benefits associated with an intervention, particularly in terms of the quantity of intervention "units" delivered, the price per unit as delivered, and the monetary equivalence of many types of outcomes (Cowell, Brown, Mills, Bender, & Wedehase, 2012). Calculating a price per unit can become complicated when interventions are delivered in group formats, which is quite common in substance use intervention programs. The costs are spread across variable numbers of individuals receiving the intervention, and there is variability in the benefits gained by different individuals. Calculating a price per unit delivered is further complicated by dependence on a wide range of factors involved with delivering substance use treatment or prevention interventions: for example, costs of training staff to deliver the intervention, equipment costs, direct and indirect staff costs, costs of screening or assessment, costs of storing medications (e.g., temperature-monitored refrigeration units and lockboxes), and other resources dictated by the intervention protocol (e.g., contingency management incentives, computer technology for client self-report and self-learning activities, biofeedback monitors). Program and research administration costs are typically not included as cost analysis variables (e.g., administrative assistance with scheduling appointments, measurement tools used for the research rather than clinical assessment). It is also important to exclude costs that are specific only to research activities.

Cost–effectiveness is essentially determined as a ratio of cost for each unit of effect in the measured outcomes (e.g., units of change in the quantity of substance use or percent of days abstinent per month). Cowell et al. (2012) discuss the statistical methods used in actually comparing alternative interventions (cost–effectiveness acceptability curves and the expected value of perfect information). Saleh et al. (2006) provide an example of a social work cost–effectiveness study in which case management was not a cost-effective add-on to substance use treatment. Zarkin et al. (2008) present another example of cost–effectiveness methodology in regard to the comparative effectiveness trial for alcohol use disorders called the COMBINE Study (see chapter 2). The cost–effectiveness results with regard to combined medication and medical management approaches were slightly different for the study's effectiveness-only conclusions compared to the conclusions related to avoiding heavy drinking and achieving good clinical outcomes.

Cost–benefit analyses, on the other hand, provide estimates of the gains expected as a result of a particular intervention being implemented. A cost–benefit ratio can be calculated as the estimated return on dollars for every dollar spent on the intervention. This type of analysis presumes an ability to assign monetary values to the different outcomes measured. Sidora-Arcoleo and Frick (2012) explain different methodologies for cost–effectiveness and cost–benefit analyses. Kuklinski, Briney, Hawkins, and Catalano (2012) presented an example of a cost–benefit analysis for a specific community-based preventive intervention, Communities That Care. In this randomized controlled trial, estimated cost savings were associated with the intervention's effects on cigarette smoking, alcohol (mis)use, and delinquency at the end of a 3-year intervention trial. The authors explain the assumptions that they applied in estimating the cost savings associated with these various outcomes.

One resource for social work investigators is the analysis of methods for conducting these sorts of analyses with regard to substance use and substance treatment services (Schori, 2011). Additional resources for informing social work investigators about the execution of cost–effectiveness research in the substance use arena are situated within a symposium report by Hilton et al. (2003). Of particular assistance is the section on improving the methodology of economic analysis of alcohol intervention studies credited to Mundt and colleagues (Hilton et al., 2003). The team enumerated five difficulties in assessing the economic effect of a treatment protocol:

- difficulties with assigning dollar values to the cost of necessary resources (as separate from the study resources)
- determining incremental costs of implementing the intervention under study versus what it would cost as a start-up program
- how to address the costs of participant attrition
- computing the power (sample sizes) needed for assessing economic impacts
- creating analytic models that generalize across trials

Comparing a treatment to a control group, they analyzed macro-level outcomes as diverse as health care–utilization costs and societal costs associated with crime and motor vehicle crashes.

IMPLEMENTATION RESEARCH

According to the NIH, implementation research involves scientifically studying the ways in which research findings, including evidence about interventions, can and do become integrated into policy and practice. Implementation research examines the behavior of professionals and support staff, organizations, consumers and their families, and policy makers as "key variables in the sustainable adoption, implementation and uptake of evidence-based interventions" (http://grants.nih.gov/grants/guide/pa-files/PAR-10-038.html#PartII).

Key issues at the implementation end of the translational research cycle relate to practical questions that influence the decision of whether or not to adopt an evidence-informed innovation and integrate it into routine practice. Glasgow (2009) suggests that these issues are similar to effectiveness research concerns: for example, how well the efficacious intervention works in real-world settings, what specific delivery conditions are associated with success, and what costs are associated with implementation. Feasibility studies may be an important step in the overall program of implementation and translational research. Social work investigators in substance use may need to engage feasibility study methodologies in order to address such issues as

- acceptability and demand for the intervention within the population being served and the service delivery settings
- capability and practicality for implementing the intervention with acceptable fidelity and integrity
- adaptations and modifications necessary to delivery
- levels of the organization involved if the intervention is to be adopted
- limited testing as an intermediate step
- assessing expansion potential if the limited testing is successful (adapted from Bowen et al., 2009)

An additional aspect of implementation research that warrants attention relates back to the intervention fidelity and integrity topic that we explored in chapter 4. Investigators may need to weigh in on the tug-of-war between fidelity to the intervention protocol and the desire for users to customize the intervention to better suit their specific circumstances (Glasgow, 2009). Such an investigation may deemphasize fidelity to specific ingredients in the intervention and emphasize adherence to the intervention's theoretical underpinnings and important principles. Or the investigation may focus on the presence of the specific ingredients essential to the intervention and have less concern about consistency with other, more modifiable components (Glasgow, 2009).

Basic research is very useful, but it should be more geared toward application than it was before.

–Luc Montagnier

SUSTAINABILITY

Finally, it is important to consider an intervention's postadoption life course. Much of our implementation and translational science focuses on the pathways to intervention uptake (see Bhattacharyya, Reeves, & Zwarenstein, 2009). Very little research is available to address how interventions are maintained over time or become discontinued, especially once external support for implementation is terminated (Rabin & Brownson, 2012). Two related areas warranting greater attention involve addressing the "assimilation gap" and "scaling up" process—what happens when an adopted intervention is not deployed widely enough and what happens when we move from implementation at a moderate scale to adoption at a large scale. Given that adoption often requires significant expenditures of scarce resources, it is important to develop an understanding of factors and processes involved with their "deadoption" as well (Massatti, Sweeney, Panzano, & Roth, 2008).

Some of the factors to consider in conducting research concerning sustainability versus deadoption of innovations include their level of organizational support and commitment, changes in the supporting evidence, risk management concerns, policy that promotes or impedes sustainability, funding for the interventions, sustainable staffing and ongoing training needs to continue its implementation, access to (technical) support, goodness-of-fit with emerging organizational or individual practitioner goals, compatibility with other programs and services being provided, whether or not a critical mass of adoption initially took place (i.e., it became routine), and the extent to which the recipients and deliverers of the intervention actually experience the gains that they expected from adoption (Aarons, Hurlburt, & Horwitz, 2011; Massatti et al., 2008). It also may be the case that a particular adopted innovation eventually will become dethroned by a newcomer with stronger or different supporting evidence. Nevertheless, substance use research will benefit from greater attention to factors involved in the sustainability of prevention and treatment interventions supported by efficacy and effectiveness studies.

CHAPTER CONCLUSIONS

There is an emerging interest among social work scholars in understanding how empirical knowledge finds its way into and is sustained in clinical practice in the community. The focus on the dissemination and implementation of science is due, at least in part, to the perception of a wide chasm between social work research and mainstream practice. The NIH has made a significant investment into the translation of science to practice, and there will be many opportunities for social work investigators to make significant contributions in this area.

Dissemination, diffusion, and implementation are three distinct aspects of moving empirical knowledge into the substance use field. Dissemination activities reflect intentional efforts to communicate new practices to a broad practice audience—those who specialize in substance use and others whose areas of focus encounter overlap with substance abuse. A number of individual and organizational factors appear to be associated with the adoption of new evidence-informed practices. The extent to which an organization feels pressure to change practices, along with the identified need for change, can influence the adoption of innovative approaches. The consistency between proposed changes and an organization's mission, goals, and objectives may also influence an adoption commitment. Individual practitioners and consumers are influenced by both the magnitude and the clinical significance of changes proffered by an innovation. While there are a number of instruments for assessing organizational and individual readiness to change substance use–related practices, only a few have a sound psychometric pedigree at this point.

Regardless of the type of change proposed, it is important to engage multiple audiences across the research endeavor. This provides an opportunity to assess perceptions of need within the communities involved and to engage constituents in developing and implementing the change processes that will affect their work and lives. The most effective adoption efforts engage providers from the outset of the research design, rather than waiting to unveil a finished product that is bereft of their input.

There is an increasing interest among program and policy decision makers in both cost–effectiveness and cost–benefit analyses. Both types of research help inform adoption and implementation decisions. There are significant challenges associated with assigning a cost both to treatment and to outcomes but also useful frameworks available for doing so.

Implementation research is the study of how findings became integrated into routine practice. This area of inquiry is concerned with the feasibility of innovative methodologies at the community practice level. Questions of intervention fidelity also fall under the heading of implementation research, including the push–pull between the local practice context and rigid implementation of the intervention. Finally, sustainability is a critical area of inquiry in implementation research. Coming to understand how substance use–related practices are retained, or not, following the departure of the research team can yield significant insight for advancing the evidence base of substance use research.

Appendix A
Alphabetical List of Journals
Commonly Presenting Substance
Abuse Research Content

Title of Journal/Periodical and Source

Addiction (formerly *British Journal on Addiction*) [Society for the Study of
  Addiction to Alcohol and Other Drugs; Wiley-Blackwell]
  http://www.addictionjournal.org/

Addiction Biology [Wiley-Blackwell]
  http://www.blackwellpublishing.com/journal.asp?ref=1355-6215

Addiction Research and Theory [Informa Healthcare]
  http://informahealthcare.com/loi/art

Addictive Behaviors: An International Journal [Elsevier]
  http://www.journals.elsevier.com/addictive-behaviors/

Alcohol [Elsevier]
  http://www.elsevier.com/wps/find/journaldescription.cws_home/525453/
  description

Alcohol Alert [National Institute on Alcohol Abuse and Alcoholism]
  http://www.niaaa.nih.gov/Publications/AlcoholAlerts/Pages/default.aspx

Alcohol and Alcoholism [Medical Council on Alcohol, Oxford University Press]
  http://www.oxfordjournals.org/our_journals/alcalc/about.html

Alcohol Research & Health [National Institute on Alcohol Abuse and
  Alcoholism]
  http://www.niaaa.nih.gov/Publications/AlcoholResearch/Pages/default.aspx

Alcoholism: Clinical and Experimental Research (ACER) [Research Society on Alcoholism; International Society for Biomedical Research on Alcoholism; Wiley-Blackwell]
http://www.blackwellpublishing.com/journal.asp?ref=0145-6008

Alcoholism Treatment Quarterly [Taylor & Francis]
http://www.tandfonline.com/loi/watq20

American Journal on Addictions (AJA) [American Academy of Addiction Psychiatry; Wiley-Blackwell]
http://www2.aaap.org/about-aaap/-american-journal-addictions

Contemporary Drug Problems: An Interdisciplinary Quarterly [Federal Legal Publications, Inc.]
http://www.federallegalpublications.com/contemporary-drug-problems

Drug and Alcohol Dependence: An International Journal on Biomedical and Psychosocial Approaches [College on Problems of Drug Dependence (CPDD); Elsevier]
http://www.elsevier.com/wps/find/journaldescription.cws_home/506052/description

Drug and Alcohol Review [Australasian Professional Society on Alcohol and other Drugs; Wiley-Blackwell]
http://www.wiley.com/bw/journal.asp?ref=0959-5236

Drug Dependence, Alcohol Abuse and Alcoholism [Excerpta Medica Abstract Journal; Elsevier]
http://www.elsevier.com/wps/find/journaldescription.cws_home/506008/description

European Addiction Research [S. Karger Publishers]
http://content.karger.com/ProdukteDB/produkte.asp?Aktion=JournalHome&ProduktNr=224233

Fetal Alcohol Research (formerly *Journal of FAS International—Fetal Alcohol Syndrome*) [FACE Research Network]
http://www.motherisk.org/FAR/index.jsp

International Journal of Mental Health and Addiction [Springer]
http://www.springer.com/public+health/journal/11469

Journal of Addiction Medicine [American Society of Addiction Medicine; Wolters Kluwer Health/OvidSP]
http://journals.lww.com/journaladdictionmedicine/pages/default.aspx

Journal of Addictive Diseases [American Osteopathic Academy of Addiction Medicine; Taylor & Francis]
http://www.tandfonline.com/loi/wjad20

Journal of Behavioral Health Services & Research [National Council for Community Behavioral Healthcare (NCCBH); Springer]
http://www.springer.com/public+health/journal/11414

Journal of Behavioral Medicine [Springer]
http://www.springer.com/medicine/journal/10865

Journal of Child & Adolescent Substance Abuse [Taylor & Francis]
http://www.tandfonline.com/action/aboutThisJournal?journalCode=wcas20

Journal of Drug Education [Baywood Publishing Company, Inc.]
http://www.baywood.com/Journals/PreviewJournals.asp?Id=0047-2379

Journal of Drug Issues [Florida State University; Sage Publications]
http://jod.sagepub.com/

Journal of Dual Diagnosis: Research and Practice in Substance Abuse Comorbidity
   [Taylor & Francis]
http://www.tandf.co.uk/journals/WJDD

Journal of Ethnicity in Substance Abuse (formerly Drugs & Society) [Taylor & Francis]
http://www.tandfonline.com/action/aboutThisJournal?journalCode=wesa20

Journal of Groups in Addiction & Recovery [Taylor & Francis]
http://www.tandfonline.com/toc/wgar20/current#.UoO0NF9OmvE

Journal of Health and Social Behavior [Sage]
http://hsb.sagepub.com/

Journal of Neuroscience and Behavioral Health [Academic Journals]
http://www.academicjournals.org/journal/JNBH

Journal of Psychoactive Drugs [Taylor & Francis]
http://www.tandf.co.uk/journals/UJPD

Journal of Social Work Practice in the Addictions [Taylor & Francis/Routledge]
http://www.tandf.co.uk/journals/WSWP

Journal of Studies on Alcohol and Drugs (formerly *Journal of Studies on Alcohol*)
   [Rutgers Center of Alcohol Studies]
http://www.jsad.com/

Journal of Substance Abuse Treatment [Elsevier]
http://www.elsevier.com/wps/find/journaldescription.cws_home/525475/
   description

Journal of Teaching in the Addictions (merged into *Substance Abuse*, see below)
   [International Coalition for Addiction Studies Education (INCASE); Taylor &
   Francis/Routledge]
http://www.tandfonline.com/loi/WTAD20

Journal of the Society for Social Work and Research [Society for Social Work Research]
http://jsswr.org/

Mental Health and Substance Use [Taylor & Francis/Routledge]
http://www.tandfonline.com/toc/rmhs20/current#.UoO1DF9OmvE

Prevention Researcher [Integrated Research Services]
http://www.tpronline.org/index.cfm

Prevention Science Journal [Society for Prevention Research]
http://www.preventionresearch.org/prevention-science-journal/

Psychology of Addictive Behaviors [American Psychological Association,
Division 50, Society of Addiction Psychology]
http://www.apa.org/pubs/journals/adb/index.aspx

Research on Social Work Practice [Sage]
http://rsw.sagepub.com/

NIDA Science and Practice Perspectives/Addiction Science & Clinical Practice
[National Institute on Drug Abuse]
http://archives.drugabuse.gov/perspectives/index.html

Social Work Abstracts [NASW Press]
http://www.naswpress.org/publications/journals/swab.html

Substance Abuse [Association for Medical Education and Research in Substance
Abuse (AMERSA);Taylor & Francis]
http://www.amersa.org/abj.asp

Substance Abuse Treatment, Prevention, and Policy (SATPP) [BioMed Central/
Springer]
http://www.substanceabusepolicy.com/

Substance Use & Misuse [Informa Healthcare]
http://informahealthcare.com/loi/sum

References

Aarons, G. A., Hurlburt, M., & Horwitz, S. M. (2011). Advancing a conceptual model of evidence-based practice implementation in public service sectors. *Administration and Policy in Mental Health, 38*, 4–23.

Abraha, L., & Cusi, C. (2012). *A Cochrane handbook: Alcohol and drug misuse.* Oxford, UK: Blackwell.

Acker, W. (1982). Objective psychological changes in alcoholics after the withdrawal of alcohol. *British Medical Bulletin, 38*(1), 95–98.

Ager, R., Roahen-Harrison, S., Toriello, P., Kissinger, P., Morse, P., Morse, E., et al. (2011). Predictors of adopting motivational enhancement therapy. *Research on Social Work Practice, 21*(1), 65–76.

Alemagno, S. A. (2009). Next generation researchers—Drug abuse research: A shifting paradigm. *Journal of Drug Issues, 39*(1), 223–226.

Allen, J. P., & Wilson, V. B. (2003). *Assessing alcohol problems: A guide for clinicians and researchers* (2nd ed.). *NIAAA Treatment Handbook Series* 4. Bethesda, MD: National Institute on Alcohol Abuse and Alcoholism.

Allison, P. D. (1995). *Survival analysis using SAS®: A practical guide.* Cary, NC: SAS Institute.

Allison, P. D. (2005). *Fixed effects regression methods for longitudinal data using SAS.* Cary, NC: SAS Institute.

American Psychiatric Association. (2000). *Diagnostic and Statistical Manual of Mental Disorders* (4th ed., text rev.). Arlington, VA: Author.

American Psychiatric Association. (2013). *Diagnostic and Statistical Manual of Mental Disorders* (5th ed.). Arlington, VA: Author.

Amodeo, M., & Fassler, I. (2000). Social workers and substance-abusing clients: Caseload composition and competency self-ratings. *American Journal of Drug and Alcohol Abuse, 26*, 629–641.

Amodeo, M., Fassler, I., & Griffin, M. (2002). MSWs with and without long-term substance abuse training: Agency, community, and personal outcomes. *Substance Abuse, 23*, 3–16.

Amodeo, M., Storti, S. A., & Larson, M. J. (2010). Moving empirically supported practices to addiction treatment programs: Recruiting supervisors to help in technology transfer. *Substance Use & Misuse, 45*(6), 968–982.

Annis, H. M., Turner, N. E., & Sklar, S. M. (1997). *Inventory of Drug-Taking Situations: User's Guide.* Toronto, Canada: Addiction Research Foundation, Centre for Addiction and Mental Health.

Anton, R. F., Moak, D. H., & Latham, P. (1995). The Obsessive Compulsive Drinking Scale: A self-rated instrument for the quantification of thoughts about alcohol and drinking behavior. *Alcoholism: Clinical & Experimental Research, 19*(1), 92–99.

Anton, R., O'Malley, S., Ciraula, D., Cisler, R., Couper, D., Donovan, D., et al. (2006). Combined pharmacotherapies and behavioral interventions for alcohol dependence: the COMBINE study: a randomized controlled trial. *JAMA, 295*(17), 2003–2017.

Armistead, L. P., Clark, H., Barber, C. N., Dorsey, S., Hughley, J., Favors, M., et al. (2004). Participant retention in the Parents Matter! program: Strategies and outcomes. *Journal of Child and Family Studies, 13*(1), 67–80.

Babor, T., Hofmann, M., Del Boca, F., Hesselbrock, V., Meyer, R., Dolinsky, Z., et al. (1992). Types of alcoholics: Evidence for an empirically derived typology based on indicators of vulnerability and severity. *Archives of General Psychiatry, 49*, 599–608.

Babor, T. F., Higgins-Biddle, J. C., Saunders, J. B., & Monteiro, M. G. (2001). *AUDIT: The Alcohol Use Disorders Identification Test. Guidelines for use in primary health care* (2nd ed.). Geneva, Switzerland: World Health Organization. Retrieved March 11, 2012, from http://whqlibdoc.who.int/hq/2001/WHO_MSD_MSB_01.6a.pdf

Babor, T. F., Kranzler, H. R., & Lauerman, R. J. (1989). Early detection of harmful alcohol consumption: Comparison of clinical, laboratory, and self-report screening procedures. *Addictive Behaviors, 14*(2), 139–157.

Babor, T. F., Stenberg, K., Anton, R., & Del Boca, F. (2000). Talk is cheap: Measuring drinking in clinical trials. *Journal of Studies on Alcohol, 61*, 55–63.

Babor, T. F., Stenius, K., Savva, S., & O'Reilly, J. (Eds.). (2008). *Publishing addiction science: A guide for the perplexed* (2nd ed.). Essex, UK: Multi-Science. Retrieved October 23, 2012, from http://www.parint.org/isajewebsite/isajebook2.htm

Backer, T. E. (1995). Assessing and enhancing readiness for change: Implications for technology transfer. In T. E. Backer, S. L. David, & G. Soucy (Eds.), *Reviewing the behavioral science knowledge base on technology transfer* (pp. 21–41). NIDA Research Monograph 155, NIH Publication 95-4035. Rockville, MD: National Institute on Drug Abuse.

Backer, T. E., Liberman, R. P., & Kuehnel, T. G. (1986). Dissemination and adoption of innovative psychosocial interventions [Electronic version]. *Journal of Consulting and Clinical Psychology, 54*(1), 111–118.

Baer, J. S., Ball, S. A., Campbell, B. K., Miele, G. M., Schoener, E. P., & Tracy, K. (2007). Training and fidelity monitoring of behavioral interventions in multi-site addictions research: A review. *Drug and Alcohol Dependence, 87*(2/3), 107–118.

Baron, R. M., & Kenny, D. A. (1986). The moderator–mediator variable distinction in social psychological research: Conceptual, strategic, and statistical considerations. *Journal of Personality and Social Psychology, 51*, 1173–1182.

Barth, R. P., Lee, B. R., Lindsey, M. A., Collins, K. S., Strieder, F., Chorpita, B. F., et al. (2012). Evidence-based practice at a crossroads: The timely emergence of common elements and common factors. *Research on Social Work Practice, 22*(1), 108–119.

Barton, W., Watkins, M., & Jarjoura, R. (1997). Youths and communities: Toward comprehensive strategies for youth development. *Social Work, 42*(5), 483–493.

Basu, D., Ball, S., Feinn, R., Gelernter, J., & Kranzler, H. (2004). Typologies of drug dependence: Comparative validity of a multivariate and four univariate models. *Drug and Alcohol Dependence, 73*, 289–300.

Bauer, D. J., Preacher, K. J., & Gil, K. M. (2006). Conceptualizing and testing random indirect effects and moderated mediation in multilevel models: New procedures and recommendations. *Psychological Methods, 11*, 142–163.

Begg, M. D., & Parides, M. K. (2003). Separation of individual-level and cluster-level covariate effects in regression analysis of correlated data [Electronic version]. *Statistics in Medicine, 22*, 2591–2602.

Begun, A. L., Berger, L. K., Otto-Salaj, L. L., & Rose, S. J. (2010). Developing effective social work university–community research collaborations. *Social Work, 55*(1), 54–62.

Begun, A. L., Berger, L. K., & Salm Ward, T. C. (2011). Using a lifecourse context for exploring alcohol change attempts and treatment efforts among individuals with alcohol dependency. *Journal of Social Work Practice in the Addictions, 11*(2), 101–123.

Begun, A. L., & Brown, S. (2013). Neurobiology of substance use disorders and implications for treatment. In S. L. A. Straussner (Ed.), *Clinical work with substance abusing clients* (3rd ed.). New York: Guilford Press.

Begun, A. L., Rose, S. J., LeBel, T. P., & Teske-Young, B. A. (2009). Implementing substance abuse screening and brief motivational intervention with women in jail. *Journal of Social Work Practice in the Addictions, 9*(1), 113–131.

Berger, L., Begun, A., & Otto-Salaj, L. (2009). Participant recruitment in intervention research: Scientific integrity and cost-effective strategies. *International Journal of Social Research Methodology, 12*(1), 79–92.

Berger, L. K., Fendrich, M., Chen, H. Y., Arria, A. M., & Cisler, R. A. (2010). Sociodemographic correlates of energy drink consumption with and without alcohol: Results of a community sample. *Addictive Behaviors, 36*(5), 516–519.

Berger, L. K., Otto-Salaj, L. L. Stoffel, V. C., Hernandez-Meier, J., & Gromoske, A. N. (2009). Barriers and facilitators of transferring research to practice: An exploratory case study of motivational interviewing. *Journal of Social Work Practice in the Addictions, 9*(2), 145–162.

Bhattacharyya, O., Reeves, S., & Zwarenstein, M. (2009). What is implementation research? Rationale, concepts, and practices. *Research on Social Work Practice, 19*(5), 491–502.

Bierman, T., Reulback, U., Lenz, B., Mucshler, M., Sperling, W., Hillemacher, T., et al. (2009). Herp mRNA expression in patients classified according to Lesch's typology. *Alcohol, 43,* 91–95.

Bina, R., Harnek Hall, D. M., Mollette, A., Smith-Osborne, A., Yum, J., Sowbel, L., et al. (2008). Substance abuse training and perceived knowledge: Predictors of perceived preparedness to work in substance abuse. *Journal of Social Work Education, 44,* 7–20.

Bischof, G., Rumpf, H. J., Meyers, C., Hapke, U., & John, U. (2005). Influence of psychiatric comorbidity in alcohol-dependent subjects in a representative population survey on treatment utilization and natural recovery [Electronic version]. *Addiction, 100*(3), 405–413.

Bliss, D. L., & Pecukonis, E. (2009). Screening and brief intervention practice model for social workers in non-substance-abuse practice settings [Electronic version]. *Journal of Social Work Practice in the Addictions, 9*(1), 21–40.

Bogenschutz, M., Tonigan, S., & Miller, W. (2006). Examining the effects of alcoholism typology and AA attendance as a mechanism of change. *Journal of Studies on Alcohol, 67*(4), 562–567.

Bogenschutz, M., Tonigan, S., & Pettinati, H. (2009). Effects of alcoholism typology on response to Naltrexone in the COMBINE study. *Alcoholism: Clinical & Experimental Research, 33*(1), 10–18.

Bond, G., Drake, R., McHugo, G., Rapp, C., & Whitley, R. (2009). Strategies for improving fidelity in the National Evidence-Based Practices Project. *Research on Social Work Practice, 19*(5), 569–581.

Borelli, B. (2011). The assessment, monitoring, and enhancement of treatment fidelity in public health clinical trials. *Journal of Public Health Dentistry, 71,* S52–S63.

Boslaugh, S. (2007). *Secondary data sources for public health: A practical guide.* Cambridge, UK: Cambridge University Press.

Bowen, C. R., & Harvey, P. D. (2006). Administration and interpretation of the Trail Making Test [Electronic version]. *Nature Protocols, 1*, 2277–2281.

Bowen, D. J., Kreuter, M., Spring, B., Cofta-Woerpel, L., Linnan, L., Weiner, D., et al. (2009). How we design feasibility studies. *American Journal of Preventive Medicine, 36*(5), 452–457.

Bradley, K. A., Boyd-Wickizer, J., Powell, S. H., & Burman, M. L. (1998). Alcohol screening questionnaires in women: A critical review. *Journal of the American Medical Association, 280*(2), 166–171.

Braver, S. L., & Smith, M. C. (1996). Maximizing both external and internal validity in longitudinal true experiments with voluntary treatments: The "combined modified" design. *Evaluation & Program Planning, 19*(4), 287–300.

Brekke, J. S., Ell, K., & Palinkas, L. A. (2007). Translational science at the National Institute of Mental Health: Can social work take its rightful place? *Research on Social Work Practice, 17*, 123–133.

Bronfenbrenner, U. (1979). *The ecology of human development.* Cambridge, MA: Harvard University Press.

Bronfenbrenner, U. (2005). *Making human beings human: Bioecological perspectives on human development.* Thousand Oaks, CA: Sage.

Bronson, D. E., & Davis, T. S. (2011). *Finding and evaluating evidence: Systematic reviews and evidence-based practice. Pocket Guides to Social Work Research Methods.* New York: Oxford University Press.

Broome, K., Flynn, P., Knight, D., & Simpson, D. (2007). Program structure, staff perceptions, and client engagement in treatment. *Journal of Substance Abuse Treatment, 33*(2), 149–158.

Brownson, R. C., Colditz, G. A., & Proctor, E. K. (Eds.). (2012). *Dissemination and implementation research in health: Translating science to practice.* New York: Oxford University Press.

Brown, S. A., Christiansen, B. A. & Goldman, M. S. (1987). The Alcohol Expectancy Questionnaire: An instrument for the assessment of adolescent and adult alcohol expectancies. *Journal of Studies on Alcohol, 48*, 483–491.

Buck, J. A. (2011). The looming expansion and transformation of public substance abuse treatment under the Affordable Care Act [Electronic version]. *Health Affairs, 30*(8), 1402–1410.

Burke, A. C., & Gregoire, T. K. (2007). Substance abuse treatment outcomes for coerced and noncoerced clients. *Health & Social Work, 32*(1), 7–15.

Burlew, A. K., Feaster, D., Brecht, M. L., & Hubbard, R. (2007). Measurement and data analysis in research addressing health disparities in substance abuse. *Journal of Substance Abuse Treatment, 36*, 25–43.

Cady, M., Winters, K. C., Jordan, D. A., Solberg, K. B., & Stinchfield, R. D. (1996). Motivation to change as a predictor of treatment outcome for adolescent substance abusers. *Journal of Child and Adolescent Substance Abuse, 5,* 73–91.

Callaghan, R., Hathaway, A., Cunningham, J., Vettese, L., Wyatt, S., & Taylor, L. (2005). Does stage-of-change predict dropout in a culturally diverse sample of adolescents admitted to inpatient substance-abuse treatment? A test of the transtheoretical model. *Addictive Behaviors, 30,* 1834–1847.

Campbell, C., Hahn, R., Elder, R., Brewer, R., Chattopadhyay, S., Fielding, J., et al. (2007). The effectiveness of limiting alcohol outlet density as a means of reducing excessive alcohol consumption and alcohol-related harms. *American Journal of Preventive Medicine, 37*(6), 557–659.

Carlson, R., Siegal, H., & Falck, R. (1995). Qualitative research methods in drug abuse and AIDS prevention research: An overview. *NIDA Research Monograph, 157,* 6–26.

Carroll, K. M., Nich, C., Sifry, R. L., Nuro, K. F., Frankforter, T. L., Ball, S. A., et al. (2000). A general system for evaluating therapist adherence and competence in psychotherapy research in the addictions. *Drug and Alcohol Dependence, 57*(3), 225–238.

Carroll, K. M., & Rounsaville, B. J. (2003). Bridging the gap: A hybrid model to link efficacy and effectiveness research in substance abuse and treatment. *Psychiatric Services, 54,* 333–339.

Center for Substance Abuse Treatment. (2009). *Addressing suicidal thoughts and behaviors in substance abuse treatment.* Treatment Improvement Protocol (TIP) Series 50, HHS Publication No. (SMA) 09-4381. Rockville, MD: Substance Abuse and Mental Health Services Administration.

Chawla, N., Collins, S., Bowen, S., Hsu, S., Grow, J., Douglass, A., et al. (2010). The Mindfulness-Based Relapse Prevention Adherence and Competence Scale: Development, interrater reliability, and validity. *Psychotherapy Research, 20*(4), 388–397.

Cherpitel, C. J. (2000). A brief screening instrument for alcohol dependence in the emergency room: The RAPS 4. *Journal of Studies on Alcohol, 61,* 447–449.

Cherpitel, C. J., & Clark, W. B. (1995). Ethnic differences in performance of screening instruments for identifying harmful drinking and alcohol dependence in the emergency room. *Alcoholism: Clinical and Experimental Research, 19*(3), 628–634.

Choi, S., & Ryan, J. (2006). Completing substance abuse treatment in child welfare: The role of co-occuring problems and primary drug of choice. *Child Maltreatment, 4,* 313–325.

Cisler, R. A., Kowalchuk, R. K., Saunders, S. M., Zweben, A., & Trinh, H. Q. (2005). Applying clinical significance methodology to alcoholism treatment trials: Determining recovery outcome status with individual- and population-based measures. *Alcoholism: Clinical and Experimental Research,* 29(11), 1991–2000.

Cisler, R. A., & Zweben, A. (1999). Development of a composite measure for assessing alcohol treatment outcome: Operationalization and validation. *Alcoholism: Clinical and Experimental Research, 23*(2), 263–271.

Clapp, J. D., Min, J. W., Shillington, A. M., Reed, M. B., & Croff, J. K. (2008). Person and environment predictors of blood alcohol concentrations: A multi-level study of college parties. *Alcoholism: Clinical and Experimental Research, 32*(1), 100–107.

Clapp, J. D., Reed, M. B., Min, J. W., Shillington, A. M., Croff, J. M., Holmes, M. R., et al. (2009). Blood alcohol concentrations among bar patrons: A multi-level study of drinking behavior. *Drug and Alcohol Dependence, 102*(1–3), 41–48.

Clark-Hammond, G., & Gregoire, T. K. (2011). Breaking ground in treating tobacco dependence at a women's treatment center. *Journal of Social Work Practice in the Addictions, 11*(1), 1–16.

Claus, R., Kindleberger, L., & Dugan, M. (2002). Predictors of attrition in a longitudinal study of substance abusers. *Journal of Psychoactive Drugs, 34*(1), 69–74.

Clay, C., Ellis, M. A., Amodeo, M., Fassler, I., & Griffin, M. L. (2003). Recruiting a community sample of African American subjects: The nuts and bolts of a successful effort. *Families in Society, 84*(30), 396–404.

Colditz, G. A. (2012). The promise and challenges of dissemination and implementation research. In R. C. Brownson, G. A. Colditz, & E. K. Proctor (Eds.), *Dissemination and implementation research in health: Translating science to practice* (pp. 3–22). New York: Oxford University Press.

Comfort, M., Loverro, J., & Kaltenbach, K. (2000). A search for strategies to engage women in substance abuse treatment. *Social Work in Health Care, 31*(4), 59–70.

Conners, N., Grant, A., Crone, C., & Whiteside-Mansell, L. (2006). Substance abuse treatment for mothers: Treatment outcomes and the impact of length of stay. *Journal of Substance Abuse Treatment, 31*(4), 447–456.

Corrigan, P. W., Kuwabara, S. A., & O'Shaughnessy, J. (2009). The public stigma of mental illness and drug addiction: Findings from a stratified random sample [Electronic version]. *Journal of Social Work, 9*, 139–148.

Cottler, L. B. (2000). *Composite International Diagnostic Interview–Substance Abuse Module (SAM).* St. Louis, MO: Department of Psychiatry, Washington University School of Medicine.

Council for International Organizations of Medical Sciences. (2002). *International ethical guidelines for biomedical research involving human subjects.* Geneva, Switzerland: World Health Organization. Retrieved from http://www.cioms.ch/publications/guidelines/guidelines_nov_2002_blurb.htm

Cowell, A. J., Brown, J. M, Mills, M. J., Bender, R. H., & Wedehase, B. J. (2012). Cost–effectiveness analysis of motivational interviewing with feedback to reduce drinking among a sample of college students. *Journal of Studies on Alcohol and Drugs, 73*(2), 226–237.

Dane, A. V., & Schneider, B. H. (1998). Program integrity in primary and early secondary prevention: Are implementation effects out of control? *Clinical Psychology Review, 18*(1), 23–45.

Darke, S. (2010). Scales for research in the addictions. In P. G. Miller, J. Strang, & P. M. Miller (Eds.), *Addiction research methods* (pp. 127–145). Hoboken, NJ: Wiley-Blackwell.

Dattalo, P. (2008). *Determining sample size: Balancing power, precision, and practicality. Pocket Guides to Social Work Research Methods.* New York: Oxford University Press.

Dattalo, P. (2010). *Strategies to approximate random sampling and assignment. Pocket Guides to Social Work Research Methods.* New York: Oxford University Press.

D'Aunno, T. (2006). The role of organization and management in substance abuse treatment: Review and roadmap. *Journal of Substance Abuse Treatment, 31,* 221–233.

D'Aunno, T., & Price, R. (2009). *National Drug Abuse Treatment System Survey, Waves II–IV.* ICPSR04146-v1. Ann Arbor, MI: Inter-university Consortium for Political and Social Research, 2009-07-30.

Dearing, J. W. (2008). Evolution of diffusion and dissemination theory. *Journal of Public Health Management and Practice, 14*(2), 99–108.

Dearing, J. W. (2009). Applying diffusion of innovation theory to intervention development. *Research on Social Work Practice, 19*(5), 503–518.

Decker, J. T., Brenner, M., & Murtagh, M. (2005). Are baccalaureate level social workers who graduate from accredited BSW programs prepared to enter into positions working in alcohol and other drug treatment programs? *Journal of Social Work in Disability and Rehabilitation, 4,* 25–38.

Dennis, M., Scott, C., & Funk, R. (2003). An experimental evaluation of recovery management checkups (RMC) for people with chronic substance use disorders. *Evaluation and Program Planning, 26,* 339–352.

Dennis, M., Titus, J., White, M., Unsicker, J., & Hodgkins, D. (2002). *Global Appraisal of Individual Needs (GAIN): Administration guide for the GAIN and related measures.* Bloomington, IL: Chestnut Health Systems.

Dennis, M., White, M., Titus, J., & Unsicker, J. (2008). *Global Appraisal of Individual Needs: Administration guide for the GAIN and related measures.* Normal, IL: Chestnut Health Systems.

Dennis, M. L., Feeny, T., & Stevens, L. H. (2006). *Global Appraisal of Individual Needs Short Screener (GAIN-SS): Administration and scoring manual for the*

GAIN-SS version 2.0.1. Bloomington, IL: Chestnut Health Systems. Retrieved from http://www.gaincc.org/_data/files/Instruments%20and%20Reports/Instruments%20Manuals/GAIN-SS%20Manual_2.0.3.pdf

DiClemente, C. C. (2006). Natural change and the troublesome use of substances: A life-course perspective. In W. R. Miller & K. M. Carroll (Eds.), *Rethinking substance abuse: What the science shows and what we should do about it* (pp. 81–96). New York: Guilford Press.

DiClemente, C. C., Carbonari, J. P., Montgomery, R. P. G., &, Hughes, S. O. (1994). The Alcohol Abstinence Self-Efficacy Scale. *Journal of Studies on Alcohol, 55*(2), 141–148.

DiClemente, C. C., & Hughes, S. O. (1990). Stages of change profiles in alcoholism treatment. *Journal of Substance Abuse, 2,* 217–235.

DiNitto, D. M., Webb, D. K., & Rubin, A. (2002). The effectiveness of an integrated treatment approach for clients with dual diagnoses. *Research on Social Work Practice, 12*(5), 621–641.

Dobson, L., & Cook, T. (1980). Avoiding Type III error in program evaluation: Results from a field experiment. *Evaluation and Program Planning, 3,* 269–276.

Doweiko, H. E. (2009). *Concepts of chemical dependency* (7th ed.). Belmont, CA: Brooks/Cole Cengage Learning.

Duka, T., Townshend, J. M., Collier, K., & Stephens, D. N. (2003). Impairments in cognitive functions after multiple detoxifications in alcoholic inpatients. *Alcoholism: Clinical and Experimental Research, 27*(10), 1563–1572.

Elvins, R., & Green, J. (2008). The conceptualization and measurement of therapeutic alliance: An empirical review. *Clinical Psychology Review, 28,* 1167–1187.

Engstrom, M., El-Bassel, N., Go, N., & Gilbert, L. (2008). Childhood sexual abuse and intimate partner violence among women in methadone treatment: A direct or mediated relationship? *Journal of Family Violence, 23,* 605–617.

Enoch, M. A. (2011). The role of early life stress as a predictor for alcohol and drug dependence. *Psychopharmacology, 214*(1), 17–31.

Epstein, E. E., Drapkin, M. L., Yusko, D. A., Cook, S. M., McCrady, B. S., & Jensen, N. K. (2005). Is alcohol assessment therapeutic? Pretreatment change in drinking among alcohol-dependent women. *Journal of Studies on Alcohol, 66*(3), 369–378.

Epstein, I. (2010). *Clinical Data-Mining: Integrating Practice and Research. Pocket Guides to Social Work Research Methods.* New York: Oxford University Press.

Evans, E., Li, L., & Hser, Y. I. (2009). Client and program factors associated with dropout from court mandated drug treatment. *Evaluation and Program Planning, 32*(3), 204–212.

Ewing, J. A. (1984). Detecting alcoholism: The CAGE questionnaire. *Journal of the American Medical Association, 252,* 1905–1907.

Ferri, M., Amato, L., & Davoli, M. (2006). Alcoholics Anonymous and other 12-step programmes for alcohol dependence [Electronic version]. *Cochrane Database of Systematic Reviews, 3*, CD005032.

Fillmore, M. T., & Jude, R. (2011). Defining binge drinking as five drinks per occasion or drinking to a.08% BAC: Which is more sensitive to risk? *American Journal on Addictions, 20*, 468–475.

Fisher, G. L., & Roget, N. A. (2009). *Encyclopedia of Substance Abuse Prevention, Treatment, and Recovery.* Thousand Oaks, CA: Sage.

Flannery, B. A., Volpicelli, J. R., & Pettinati, H. M. (1999). Psychometric properties of the Penn Alcohol Craving Scale. *Alcoholism: Clinical and Experimental Research, 23*(8), 1289–1295.

Fogel, S. J., & Roberts-DeGennaro, M. (2011). Introduction. In M. Roberts-DeGennaro & S. J. Fogel (Eds.), *Using evidence to inform practice for community and organizational change* (pp. xix–xxv). Chicago: Lyceum Books.

Folstein, M. F., Folstein, S. E., & McHugh, P. R. (1975). Mini-Mental State: A practical method for grading the state of patients for the clinician. *Journal of Psychiatric Research, 12*, 189–198.

Fraser, J. S., & Solovey, A. D. (2007). Chemical dependency. In J. S. Fraser & A. D. Solovey (Eds.), *Second-order change in psychotherapy: The golden thread that unifies effective treatments* (pp. 287–317). Washington, DC: American Psychological Association.

Fraser, M. W., Richman, J. M., Galinsky, M. J., & Day, S. H. (2009). *Intervention research: Developing social programs. Pocket Guides to Social Work Research Methods.* New York: Oxford University Press.

Friedman, A. S., & Utada, A. (1989). A method for diagnosis and planning the treatment of adolescent drug abusers (the Adolescent Drug Abuse Diagnosis [ADAD] instrument). *Journal of Drug Education, 19*(4), 285–312.

Friedmann, P., Durkin, E., Lemon, S., & D'Aunno, T. (2003a). Trends in comprehensive service availability in outpatient drug abuse treatment. *Journal of Substance Abuse Treatment, 24*, 81–88.

Friedmann, P., Lemon, S., Stein, M., & D'Aunno, T. (2003b). Community referral sources and entry of treatment-naive clients into outpatient addiction treatment. *American Journal of Drug and Alcohol Abuse, 29*, 105–115.

Fritz, C. O., Morris, P. E., & Richler, J. J. (2012). Effect size estimates: Current use, calculations, and interpretation. *Journal of Experimental Psychology: General, 141*(1), 2–18.

Fritz, M. S., & MacKinnon, D. P. (2007). Required sample size to detect the mediated effect. *Psychological Science, 18*(3), 233–239.

Fry, C., & Dwyer, R. (2001). For love or money? An exploratory study of why injecting drug users participate in research. *Addiction, 96*, 1319–1325.

Fry, C. L., Hall, W., Ritter, A., & Jenkinson, R. (2006). The ethics of paying drug users who participate in research: A review and practical recommendations. *Journal of Empirical Research on Human Research Ethics: An International Journal, 1*(4), 21–36.

Gambrill, E. (2004). Contributions of critical thinking and evidence-based practice to the fulfillment of the ethical obligations of professionals. In H. E. Briggs & T. L. Rzepnicki (Eds.), *Using evidence in social work practice: Behavioral perspectives* (pp. 3–19). Chicago: Lyceum Books.

Garbarino, J., & Abramowitz, R. H. (1992). The ecology of human development. In J. Garbarino (Ed.), *Children and families in the social environment* (2nd ed., pp. 11–35). New York: Aldine de Gruyter.

Garfield, R. L., Lave, J. R., & Donohue, J. M. (2010). Health reform and the scope of benefits for mental health and substance use disorder services. *Psychiatric Services, 61*, 1081–1086.

Garner, B., Passetti, L., Orndorff, M., & Godley, S. (2007). Reasons for and attitudes toward follow-up research participation among adolescents enrolled in an outpatient substance abuse treatment program. *Journal of Child & Adolescent Substance Abuse, 16*(4), 45–57.

Garriott, J. (1993). Drug use among homicide victims: Changing patterns. *American Journal of Forensic Medical Pathology, 14*(3), 234–237.

Gassman, R. A., Demone, H. W., & Albilal, R. (2001). Alcohol and other drug content in core courses: Encouraging substance abuse assessment. *Journal of Social Work Education, 37*, 137–145.

Giacopassi, D., & Winn, R. (1995). Alcohol availability and alcohol-related crashes: Does distance make a difference? *American Journal of Drug and Alcohol Abuse, 21*(3), 407–416.

Glasgow, R. E. (2009). Critical measurement issues in translational research. *Research on Social Work Practice, 19*(5), 560–568.

Goldman, G. D. (2009). Initial validation of a brief individual readiness for change scale (BIRCS) for use with addiction program staff practitioners. *Journal of Social Work Practice in the Addictions, 9*(2), 184–203.

Gough, D., Oliver, S., & Thomas, J. (2012). *An introduction to systematic reviews.* Thousand Oaks, CA: Sage.

Grant, J. E., & Portenza, M. N. (2005). Pathological gambling and other "behavioral" addictions. In R. J. Frances, S. I. Miller, & A. H. Mack (Eds.), *Clinical textbook of addictive disorders* (3rd ed., pp. 303–320). New York: Guilford Press.

Gray, M., Plath, D., & Webb, S. A. (2009). *Evidence-based social work: A critical stance.* New York: Routledge.

Green, C., Polen, M., Dickinson, D., Lynch, F., & Bennett, M. (2002). Gender differences in predictors of initiation, retention and completion in an HMO-based substance abuse treatment program. *Journal of Substance Abuse Treatment 23*, 285–295.

Green, L. W., Ottoson, J. M., Garcia, C., & Hiatt, R. A. (2009). Diffusion theory and knowledge dissemination, utilization, and integration in public health. *Annual Review of Public Health, 30,* 151–174.

Gregoire, T. (1996). Subtypes of alcohol involvement and their relationships to exits from homelessness. *Substance Use and Misuse, 31*(10), 1333–1357.

Gregoire, T. (2002). The validity of a social indicator approach to substance misuse needs assessment. *Substance Use and Misuse, 37*(3), 357–379.

Gregoire, T., Burke, A., Moon, S., Ginzer, L., & Joliff, A. (2006). *A social indicator approach to estimating substance abuse treatment needs in Ohio.* Columbus: Ohio Department of Alcohol and Drug Addiction Services.

Gregoire, T. K., & Burke, A. C. (2004). The relationship of legal coercion to readiness to change among adults with alcohol and other drug problems. *Journal of Substance Abuse Treatment, 26*(1), 337–343.

Guo, S. (2010). *Survival analysis. Pocket Guides to Social Work Research Methods.* New York: Oxford University Press.

Hahs-Vaughn, D. (2006). Analysis of data from complex samples. *International Journal of Research & Method in Education, 29*(2), 165–183.

Hall, E., Zuniga, R., Cartier, J., Anglin, M. D., Danila, B., Ryan, R., et al. (2003). *Staying in touch: A fieldwork manual of tracking procedures for locating substance abusers in follow-up studies,* (2nd ed.). Los Angeles: UCLA Integrated Substance Abuse Programs.

Hall, M. N., Amodeo, M., Shaffer, H. J., & VanderBilt, J. (2000). Social workers employed in substance abuse treatment agencies: A training needs assessment. *Social Work, 45*(2), 141–155.

Hansten, M., Downey, L., Rosengren, D., & Donovan, D. (2000). Relationship between follow-up rates and treatment outcomes in substance abuse research: More is better but when is "enough" enough? *Addiction, 95*(9), 1403–1416.

Harrington, M., Babbin, S., Redding, C., Burditt, C., Paiva, A., & Meier, K. (2011). Psychometric assessment of the Temptations to Try Alcohol Scale. *Addictive Behaviors, 36,* 431–433.

Harrison, L., & Gfroerer, J. (1992). The intersection of drug use and criminal behavior: Results from the National Household Survey on Drug Abuse. *Crime and Delinquency, 38*(4), 422–443.

Harrison, P. A., & Hoffman, N. G. (2001). SUDDS-IV: Administration guide. Smithfield, RI: Evince Clinical Assessments. Retrieved from http://www.evinceassessment.com/product_sudds.html

Hasin, D. S., Trautman, K., Miele, G., Samet, S., Smith, M., & Endicott, J. (1996). Psychiatric Research Interview for Substance and Mental Disorders

(PRISM): Reliability for substance abusers. *American Journal of Psychiatry*, *153*, 1195–1201.

Hawkins, D., & Catalano, R. (2002). *Investing in your community's youth: An introduction to the Communities That Care System*. South Deerfield, MI: Channing Bete.

Hawkins, J., Oesterle, S., Brown, E., Monahan, K., Abbott, R., Arthur, M., et al. (2012). Sustained decreases in risk exposure and youth problem behaviors after installation of the Communities That Care Prevention System in a randomized trial. *Archives of Pediatric Adolescent Medicine*, *66*(2), 141–148.

Heather, N. (2006). Controlled drinking, harm reduction and their roles in the response to alcohol-related problems. *Addiction Research and Theory*, *14*(1), 7–18.

Heather, N., Luce, A., Peck, D., Dunbar, B., & James, I. (1999). The development of a treatment version of the Readiness to Change Questionnaire. *Addiction Research*, *7*(1), 63–68.

Heatherton, T. F., Kozlowski, L. T., Frecker, R. C., & Fagerström, K. O. (1991). The Fagerström Test for Nicotine Dependence: A revision of the Fagerström Tolerance Questionnaire. *British Journal of Addiction J Addiction*, *86*(9), 1119-1127.

Heckathorn, D. (1997). Respondent-driven sampling: A new approach to the study of hidden populations. *Social Problems*, *44*(2), 174–199.

Herie, M., & Martin, G. W. (2002). Knowledge diffusion in social work: A new approach to bridging the gap. *Social Work*, *47*(1), 85–95.

Herscovitch, L., & Meyer, J. P. (2002). Commitment to organizational change: Extension of a three-component model. *Journal of Applied Psychology*, *87*(3), 474–487.

Hesse, M. (2006). The Readiness Ruler as a measure of readiness to change poly-drug use in drug abusers [Electronic version]. *Harm Reduction Journal*, *3*(3), 1–5.

Hesse, M., Vanderplasschen, W., Rapp, R., Broekaert, E., & Fridell, M. (2007). Case management for persons with substance use disorders. *Cochrane Database of Systematic Reviews*, *4*, CD006265.

Hesselbrock, V., & Hesselbrock, M. (2006). Are there empirically supported and clinically useful subtypes of alcohol dependence? *Addiction*, *101*(Suppl. *1*), 97–103.

Hillemacher, T., Bayerlein, K., Wilhelm, J., Bonsch, D., Poleo, D., Sperling, W., et al. (2006). Recurrent detoxifications are associated with craving in patients classified as type 1 in Lesch's typology. *Alcohol & Alcoholism*, *41*(1), 66–69.

Hilton, M. E., Fleming, M., Glick, H., Gutman, M. A., Lu, Y., McKay, J., et al. (2003). Services integration and cost–effectiveness. *Alcoholism: Clinical and Experimental Research*, *27*(2), 271–280.

Hinshaw, S. P., Hoagwood, K., Jensen, P. S., Kratochvil, C., Bickman, L., Clarke, G., et al. (2004). AACAP 2001 Research Forum: Challenges and recommendations regarding recruitment and retention of participants in research investigations. *Journal of the American Academy of Child and Adolescent Psychiatry*, 43(8), 1037–1045.

Hirsch, L. S., McCrady, B. S., & Epstein, E. E. (1997). Drinking-Related Locus of Control Scale: The factor structure with treatment-seeking outpatients. *Journal of Studies on Alcohol*, 58(2), 162–166.

Hodgins, D. C., Maticka-Tyndale, E., el-Guebaly, N., & West, M. (1993). The CAST-6: Development of a short-form of the Children of Alcoholics Screening Test. *Addictive Behavior*, 18(3), 337–345.

Hoffman, K. A., Quanbeck, A., Ford, J. H., II, Wrede, F., Wright, D., Lambert-Wacey, D., et al. (2011). Improving substance abuse data systems to measure "waiting time to treatment": Lessons learned from a quality improvement initiative [Electronic version]. *Health Informatics*, 17, 256–265.

Hoffman, N. G., & Harrison, P. A. (1995). *SUDDS-IV: Substance Use Disorder Diagnostic Schedule-IV*. St. Paul, MN: New Standards.

Holt, D. T., Armenakis, A. A., Field, H. S., & Harris, S. G. (2007). Readiness for organizational change: The systematic development of a scale. *Journal of Applied Behavioral Science*, 43(2), 232–255.

Horton, A. M., & Roberts, C. (2003). Demographic effects on the Trail Making Test in a drug abuse treatment sample. *Archives of Clinical Neuropsychology*, 18(1), 49–56.

Janson, K. J. (2004). From persistence to pursuit: A longitudinal examination of momentum during the early stages of strategic change. *Organizational Science*, 15(3), 276–294.

Jung, T., Scott, T., Davies, H., Bower, P., Whalley, D., McNally, R., et al. (2009). Instruments for exploring organizational culture: A review of the literature. *Public Administration Review*, 69(6), 1087–1096.

Kail, B. L. (2010). Motivating women with substance abuse and intimate partner violence. *Journal of Social Work Practice in the Addictions*, 10(1), 25–43.

Kakinami, L., & Conner, K. R. (2010). Sampling strategies for addiction research. In P. G. Miller, J. Strang, & P. M. Miller (Eds.), *Addiction research methods* (pp. 27–42). Ames, IA: Wiley-Blackwell/Addiction Press.

Kaminer, Y., Blitz, C., Burleson, J. A., & Sussman, J. (1998). The Teen Treatment Services Review (T-TSR). *Journal of Substance Abuse Treatment*, 15, 291–300.

Kaminer, Y., Bukstein, O. G., & Tarter, R. E. (1991). The Teen-Addiction Severity Index: Rationale and reliability. *International Journal of Addictions*, 26(2), 219–226.

Kazdin, A. E., & Nock, M. K. (2003). Delineating mechanisms of change in child and adolescent therapy: Methodological issues and research recommendations. *Journal of Child Psychology and Psychiatry, 44*(8), 1116–1129.

Kazmierczak, D. A., Smyth, N. J., & Wodarski, J. S. (1999). Screenings and assessment instruments for alcohol and other drugs. *Family Therapy, 26*(2), 103–119.

Keifer, F., Jimenez-Arriero, M., Klein, O., Diehl, A., & Rubio, G. (2007). Cloninger's typology and treatment outcome in alcohol-dependent subjects during pharmacotherapy with naltrexone. *Addiction Biology, 13*, 124–129.

Klein, C., di Menza, S., Arfken, C., & Schuster, C. R. (2002). Interaction effects of treatment setting and client characteristics on retention and completion. *Journal of Psychoactive Drugs, 34*(1), 39–50.

Kleschinsky, J., Bosworth, L., Nelson, S., Walsh, E., & Shaffer, H. (2009). Persistence pays off: Follow-up methods for difficult-to-track longitudinal samples. *Journal of Studies on Alcohol and Drugs, 70*(5), 751–761.

Kline, R. B. (2009). *Becoming a behavioral science researcher: A guide to producing research that matters.* New York: Guilford Press.

Knight, D., Becan, J., & Flynn, P. (2012). Organizational consequences of staff turnover in outpatient substance abuse treatment programs. *Journal of Substance Abuse Treatment, 42*, 143–150.

Kogoj, D., Lesch, O. M., Blüml, V., Riegler, A., Vyssoki, B., Schlaff, G., et al. (2010). Lesch alcoholism typology medical treatment and research. *Archives of Psychiatry and Psychotherapy, 4*, 37–48.

Kraemer, H., Kiernan, M., Essex, M., & Kupfer, D. (2008). How and why criteria defining moderators and mediators differ between the Baron & Kenny and MacArthur approaches. *Health Psychology, 27*, S101–S108.

Kuklinski, M. R., Briney, J. S., Hawkins, J. D., & Catalano, R. F. (2012). Cost–benefit analysis of Communities That Care outcomes at eighth grade. *Prevention Science, 13*(2), 150–161.

Lamar, B., & Reed, B. (1997). *Medical care for substance abusing women: Availability and utilization of reproductive health services in outpatient treatment units.* Ann Arbor, MI: Institute for Social Research, University of Michigan.

Landsvark, J., Brown, C. H., Chamberlain, P., Palinkas, L., Ogihara, M., Czaja, S., et al. (2012). Design and analysis in dissemination and implementation research. In R. C. Brownson, G. A. Colditz, & E. K. Proctor, (Eds.), *Dissemination and implementation research in health: Translating science to practice* (pp. 225–260). New York: Oxford University Press.

LeBel, T. P. (2010). Prisoner reentry—What corrections administrators need to know. In S. Stojkovic (Ed.), *Managing special populations in jails and prisons* (Vol. 2, pp. 1–40). Kingston, NJ: Civic Research Institute.

LeCroy, C. W., & Krysik, J. (2007). Understanding and interpreting effect size measures: A research note. *Social Work Research, 31*, 243–248.

Lee, R. E. (2009). "If you build it, they may not come": Lessons from a funded project [Electronic version]. *Research on Social Work Practice, 19,* 251–260.

Lehman, W. E., Greener, J. M., & Simpson, D. D. (2002). Assessing organizational readiness for change. *Journal of Substance Abuse Treatment, 22*(4), 197–209.

Lemieux, C. M., & Schroeder, J. (2004). Seminar on addictive disorders: An exploration of students' knowledge, attitudes, and behavior. *Journal of Social Work Practice in the Addictions, 4,* 3–21.

Littell, J. H., Corocoran, J., & Pillai, V. (2008). *Systematic reviews and meta-analysis. Pocket Guides to Social Work Research Methods.* New York: Oxford University Press.

Liu S., Siegel, P. Z., Brewer, R. D., Mokdad, A. H, Sleet, D. A., & Serdula M. (1997). Prevalence of alcohol-impaired driving. Results from a national self-reported survey of health behaviors. *JAMA, 277*(2), 122–125.

Livingston, M., Chikritzhs, T., & Room, R. (2007). Changing the density of alcohol outlets to reduce alcohol-related problems. *Drug and Alcohol Review, 26*(5), 557–566.

LoCastro, J. S., Youngblood, M., Cisler, R. A., Mattson, M. E., Zweben, A., Anton, R. F., et al. (2009). Alcohol treatment effects on secondary nondrinking outcomes and quality of life: The COMBINE study. *Journal of Studies on Alcohol and Drugs, 70*(2), 186–196.

Longabaugh, R., Donovan, D. M., Karno, M. P., McCrady, B. S., Morgensgtern, J., & Tonigan, J. S. (2005). Active ingredients: How and why evidence-based alcohol behavioral treatment interventions work. *Alcoholism: Clinical and Experimental Research, 29*(2), 235–247.

Lowman, C., Hunt, W. A., Litten, R. Z., & Drummond, D. C. (2000). Research perspectives on alcohol craving: An overview. *Addiction, 95*(Suppl. 2), S45–S54.

Lui, S., Terplan, M., & Smith, E. J. (2008). Psychosocial interventions for women enrolled in alcohol treatment during pregnancy. *Cochrane Database of Systematic Reviews, 3,* CD006753.

Lundahl, B. W., Kunz, C., Brownell, C., Tollefson, D., & Burke, B. L. (2010). A meta-analysis of motivational interviewing: Twenty-five years of empirical studies. *Research on Social Work Practice, 20*(2), 137–160.

MacKinnon, D. P. (2012). Integrating mediators and moderators in research design. *Research on Social Work Practice, 21*(6), 675–681.

MacKinnon, D. P., & Fairchild, A. J. (2009). Current directions in mediation analysis [Electronic version]. *Current Directions in Psychological Sciences, 18*(1), 16–20.

MacKinnon, D. P., Fairchild, A. J., & Fritz, M. S. (2007). Mediation analysis. *Annual Review of Psychology, 58,* 593–614.

Madson, M. B., & Campbell, T. C. (2006). Measures of fidelity in motivational enhancement: A systematic review. *Journal of Substance Abuse Treatment, 31,* 67–73.

Maisto, S. A., McKay, J. R., & Tiffany, S. T. (2004). Diagnosis. National Institute on Alcohol Abuse and Alcoholism Publications. Retrieved on February 10, 2012, from http://pubs.niaaa.nih.gov/publications/AssessingAlcohol/diagnosis.htm

Mann, R. E., Sobell, L. C., Sobell, M. B., & Sobell, D. P. (1985). Reliability of a family tree questionnaire for assessing family history of alcohol problems. *Drug and Alcohol Dependence, 15*, 61–67.

Marcus, D., Kashy, D., Wintdersteen, M., & Diamond, G. (2011). The therapeutic allinance in adolescent substance abuse treatment: A one-with-many analysis. *Journal of Counseling Psychology, 58*(3), 449–455.

Marlatt, G. A., & Witkiewitz, K. (2002). Harm reduction approaches to alcohol use: Health promotion, prevention, and treatment. *Addictive Behaviors, 27*(6), 867–886.

Marsiglia, F. F., Kulis, S., Rodriguez, G. M., Becerra, D., & Catillo, J. (2009). Culturally specific youth substance abuse resistance skills: Applicability across the U.S.–Mexico border. *Research on Social Work Practice, 19*(2), 149–151.

Martinez, K. K., & Wong, S. E. (2009). Increasing attendance at domestic violence groups with telephone and written prompts. *Research on Social Work Practice, 19*(4), 460–463.

Massatti, R. R., Sweeney, H. A., Panzano, P. C., & Roth, D. (2008). The de-adoption of innovative mental health practices (IMHP): Why organizations choose not to sustain an IMHP. *Administration and Policy in Mental Health, 35*, 50–65.

Maxwell, J. C., Podus, D., & Walsh, D. (2009). Lessons learned from the deadly sisters: Drug and alcohol treatment disruption, and consequences from Hurricanes Katrina and Rita. *Substance Use & Misuse, 44*(12), 1681–1694.

Mayer, J., & Filstead, W. J. (1979). The Adolescent Alcohol Involvement Scale: An instrument for measuring adolscents' use and misuse of alcohol. *Journal of Studies on Alcohol, 40*, 291–300.

McKay, J. R., & Hiller-Sturmhöfel, S. (2011). Treating alcoholism as a chronic disease: Approaches to long-term continuing care. *Alcohol Research & Health, 33*(4), 356–370.

McKellar, J., Kelly, J., Harris, A., & Moos, R. (2006). Pretreatment and during treatment risk factors for dropout among patients with substance use disorders. *Addictive Behaviors, 31*, 450–460.

McKenzie, M., Peterson Tulsky, J., Long, H., Chesney, H. & Moss, A. (1999). Tracking and follow-up of marginalized populations: A review. *Journal of Health Care for the Poor and Underserved, 10*(4), 409–429.

A. Thomas McLellan, James R. McKay, Robert Forman, John Cacciola & Jack Kemp (2002). Reconsidering the evaluation of addiction treatment: from retrospective follow-up to concurrent recovery monitoring. *Addiction, 100*, 447–458

McLellan, A. T. (2010). What is recovery? Revisiting the Betty Ford Institute Consensus Panel definition. *Journal of Social Work Practice in the Addictions*, *10*, 109–113.

McLellan, A. T., Alterman, A. I., Cacciloa, J., Metzger, D., & O'Brien, C. P. (1992a). A new measure of substance abuse treatment: Initial studies of the Treatment Service Review. *Journal of Nervous and Mental Disease*, *180*, 101–110.

McLellan, A. T., Cacciola, J. S., Alterman, A. I., Rikoon, S. H., & Carise, D. (2006). The Addiction Severity Index at 25: Origins, contributions and transitions. *American Journal on Addictions*, *15*(2), 113–124.

McLellan, A. T., Kushner, H., Metzger, D., Peters, R., Smith, I., Grissom, G., et al. (1992). The fifth edition of the Addiction Severity Index. *Journal of Substance Abuse Treatment*, *9*, 199–213.

McMurtry, S. L., & Hudson, W. W. (2000). The Client Satisfaction Inventory: Results of an initial validation study. *Research on Social Work Practice*, *10*, 644–663.

McMurtry, S. L., & Torres, J. B. (2002). Initial validation of a Spanish-language version of the Client Satisfaction Inventory. *Research on Social Work Practice*, *12*, 124–142.

McNeece, C. A., & DiNitto, D. M. (2012). *Chemical dependency: A systems approach* (4th ed.). Boston: Pearson.

Mee-Lee, D., McLellan, A. T., & Miller, S. D. (2010). What works in substance abuse and dependence treatment. In B. L. Duncan, S. D. Miller, B. E. Wampold, & M. A. Hubble (Eds.), *The heart & soul of change: Delivering what works in therapy* (2nd ed., pp. 393–417). Washington, DC: American Psychological Association.

Melnick, G., Wexler, H., Chaple, M., & Banks, S. (2006). The contribution of consensus within staff and client groups as well as concordance between staff and clients to treatment engagement. *Journal of Substance Abuse Treatment*, *31*, 277–285.

Mertens, J. Flisher, A., Satre, D., & Weisner, C. (2008). The role of medical conditions and primary care services in 5-year substance use outcomes among chemical dependency treatment patients. *Drug & Alcohol Dependence*, *98*, 45–53.

Meyers, K., Webb, A., Frantz, J., & Randall, M. (2003). What does it take to retain substance abusing adolescents in research protocols? Delineation of effort required, strategies undertaken, costs incurred, and 6-month post treatment differences by retention difficulty. *Drug and Alcohol Dependence*, *69*, 73–85.

Milby, J., Schumacher, J., Wallace, D., Freedman, M., & Vuchinich, R. (2005). To house or not to house: The effects of providing housing to homeless substance abusers in treatment. *American Journal of Public Health*, *95*, 1259–1265.

Miller, G. (1985). *The Substance Abuse Subtle Screening Inventory (SASSI): Manual* (2nd ed.). Springfield, IN: SASSI Institute.

Miller, L. (1985). Neuropsychological assessment of substance abusers: Review and recommendations. *Journal of Substance Abuse Treatment*, *2*, 5–17.

Miller, P., & Miller, W. (2009). What should we be aiming for in the treatment of addiction? *Addiction, 104*(5), 685–686.

Miller, P. G., Strang, J., & Miller, P. M. (2010). *Addiction research methods.* Hoboken, NJ: Wiley-Blackwell.

Miller, P. M. (Ed.) (2009). *Evidence-based addiction treatment.* Burlington, MA: Academic Press/Elsevier.

Miller, W. (1996). What is a relapse? Fifty ways to leave the wagon. *Addiction, 91*(Suppl.), S15–S27.

Miller, W., & Carroll, K. (2006). *Rethinking substance abuse: What the science shows and what we should do about it.* New York: Guilford Press.

Miller, W. R., & del Boca, F. K. (1994). Measurement of drinking behavior using the Form 90 family of instruments. *Journal of Studies on Alcohol and Drugs, 12*(Suppl.), 112–118.

Miller, W. R., Forcehimes, A. A., & Zweben, A. (2011). *Treating addictions: A guide for professionals.* New York: Guilford Press.

Miller, W. R., & Manuel, J. K. (2008). How large must a treatment effect be before it matters to practitioners? An estimation method and demonstration. *Drug and Alcohol Review, 27*, 524–528.

Miller, W. R., & Tonigan, J. S. (1996). Assessing drinkers' motivation for change: The Stages of Change Readiness and Treatment Eagerness Scale (SOCRATES). *Psychology of Addictive Behaviors, 10*(2), 81–89.

Miller, W. R., Tonigan, J. S., & Longabaugh, R. (1995). The Drinker Inventory of Consequences (DrInC): An instrument for assessing adverse consequences of alcohol abuse. Test manual. (Vol. 4). Project MATCH Monograph Series. Rockville, MD: National Institute on Alcohol Abuse and Alcoholism.

Milligan, C., Nich, C., & Carroll, K. (2004). Ethnic differences in substance abuse treatment retention, compliance, and outcome from two clinical trials. *Psychiatric Services, 55*(2), 167–173.

Minton, T. D. (2011). *Jail inmates at midyear 2010—Statistical tables.* NCJ 233431. Washington, DC: US Bureau of Justice, Office of Justice Programs, Bureau of Justice Statistics. Retrieved September 1, 2011, from http://bjs.ojp.usdoj.gov/content/pub/pdf/jim10st.pdf

Mitchell, O., Wilson, D. B., & MacKenzie, D. L. (2006). *The effectiveness of incarceration-based drug treatment on criminal behavior.* Campbell Systematic Reviews, 2006:11.

Moore, B. (2005). Empirically supported family and peer interventions for dual disorders. *Research on Social Work Practice, 15*(4), 231–245.

Moreira, M. T., Smith, L. A., & Foxcroft, D. (2009). Social norms interventions to reduce alcohol misuse in University or College students. *Cochrane Database of Systematic Reviews, 3*, CD006748.

Moss, H. B., Chen, C. M., & Yi, H. Y. (2007). Subtypes of alcohol dependence in a nationally representative sample. *Drug and Alcohol Dependence, 91,* 149–158.

Mossakowski, K. (2008). Is the duration of poverty and unemployment a risk factor for heavy drinking? *Social Science & Medicine, 67*(6), 947–955.

Moyers, T. B., Martin, T., Manuel, J. K., Hendrickson, S. M. L., & Miller, W. R. (2005). Assessing competence in the use of motivational interviewing. *Journal of Substance Abuse Treatment, 28*(1), 19–26.

Murray, D. M. (1998). *Design and analysis of group-randomized trials. Monographs in Epidemiology and Biostatistics* (Vol. 27). New York: Oxford University Press.

Naleppa, M. J., & Cagle, J. G. (2010). Treatment fidelity in social work intervention research: A review of published studies. *Research on Social Work Practice, 20*(6), 674–681.

National Academy of Science. (2009). *On being a scientist: A guide to responsible research* (3rd ed.). Retrieved from http://www.nap.edu/catalog.php?record_id=12192

National Institute on Alcohol Abuse and Alcoholism. (2001). Alcohol Alert #53: Cognitive impairment and recovery from alcoholism. Retrieved March 11, 2012, from http://pubs.niaaa.nih.gov/publications/aa53.htm

National Institute on Alcohol Abuse and Alcoholism. (2003a). Assessing Alcohol Problems: A Guide for Clinicians and Researchers, Second Edition. NIH Publication No. 03-3745. Retrieved November 4, 2013 from http://pubs.niaaa.nih.gov/publications/AssessingAlcohol/

National Institute on Alcohol Abuse and Alcoholism. (2003b). Task Force on Recommended Alcohol Questions—National Council on Alcohol Abuse and Alcoholism recommended sets of alcohol consumption questions–October 15–16, 2003. Retrieved March 11, 2012, from http://www.niaaa.nih.gov/research/guidelines-and-resources/recommended-alcohol-questions

National Institute on Alcohol Abuse and Alcoholism. (2010). Celebrating 40 years of alcohol research. *Alcohol Research & Health, 33*(1–2). Retrieved September 15, 2012, from http://alcoholreports.blogspot.com/2010/08/celebrating-40-years-of-alcohol.html

National Institute on Alcohol Abuse and Alcoholism. (2011). *Women and alcohol.* Retrieved January 9, 2013, from http://pubs.niaaa.nih.gov/publications/womensfact/womensfact.htm

National Institute on Drug Abuse. (2006). *Women & substance abuse.* Retrieved on November 15, 2013, from http://archives.drugabuse.gov/newsroom/06/NS-10.html

National Institutes of Health. (1999). Bridging science and service: A report by the National Advisory Mental Health Council's Clinical Treatment and Services Research Workgroup. Bethesda, MD: National Institutes of Health,

National Institute of Mental Health. Retrieved November 15, 2013, from http://wwwapps.nimh.nih.gov/ecb/archives/nimbridge.pdf

Norcross, J. C., Krebs, P. M., & Prochaska, J. O. (2011). Stages of change [Electronic version]. *Journal of Clinical Psychology: In Session, 67*(2), 143–154.

Norström, T. (2004). Per capita alcohol consumption and all-cause mortality in Canada, 1950–98. *Addiction, 99*(10), 1274–1278.

Nugent, W. R. (2010). *Analyzing single system design data.* Pocket Guides to Social Work Research Methods. New York: Oxford University Press.

Nyamathi, A., Leake, B., Longshore, D., & Gelberg, L. (2001). Reliability of homeless women's reports: Concordance between hair assay and self report of cocaine use. *Nursing Research, 50*(3), 165–171.

O'Brien, M. C., McCoy, T. P., Rhodes, S. D., Wagoner, A., & Wolfson, M. (2008). Caffeinated cocktails: Energy drink consumption, high-risk drinking, and alcohol-related consequences among college students. *Academic Emergency Medicine, 15*(5), 453–460.

O'Hare, T. (2001). The Drinking Context Scale: A confirmatory analysis. *Journal of Substance Abuse Treatment, 20,* 129–136.

Oei, T. P. S., Hasking, P. A., & Young, R. (2005). Drinking refusal self-efficacy questionnaire-revised (DRSEQ-R): A new factor structure with confirmatory factor analysis. *Drug and Alcohol Dependence, 78*(3), 297–307.

Padgett, D. K. (2008). *Qualitative methods in social work research,* (2nd ed.). Thousand Oaks, CA: Sage.

Pandey, S., & Elliott, W. (2010). Suppressor variables in social work research: Ways to identify in multiple regression models. *Journal of the Society for Social Work and Research, 1*(1), 28–40.

Pates, R., & Riley, D. (Eds.). (2012). *Harm reduction in substance use and high-risk behavior: International policy and practice.* West Sussex, UK: Wiley-Blackwell/ Addiction Press.

Patterson, D. A., & McKiernan, P. M. (2010). Organizational and clinical implications of integrating an alcohol screening and brief intervention within non-substance abuse serving agencies. *Journal of Evidence-Based Social Work, 7,* 332–347.

Prat, G., Adan, A., Pérez-Pàmies, M., & Sànchez-Turet, M. (2008). Neurocognitive effects of alcohol hangover. *Addictive Behaviors, 33*(1), 15–23.

Prochaska, J. O., DiClemente, C. C., & Norcross, J. C. (1992). In search of how people change: Applications to addictive behaviors. *American Psychologist, 47*(9), 1102–1114.

Proctor, E. K., & Rosen, A. (2008). From knowledge production to implementation: Research challenges and imperatives. *Research on Social Work Practice, 18*(4), 285–291.

Project MATCH Research Group. (1998). Matching alcoholism treatments to client heterogeneity: Project MATCH three-year drinking outcomes. *Alcoholism: Clinical and Experimental Research, 22*(6), 1300–1311.

Purshouse, R., Meier, P., Brennan, A., Taylor, K., & Rachid, R. (2010). Estimated effect of alcohol pricing policies on health and health economic outcomes in England: An epidemiological model. *The Lancet, 375*(9723), 17–23.

Quinn, G. (2010). Institutional denial or minimization: Substance abuse training in social work education. *Substance Abuse, 31*, 8–11.

Rabin, B. A., & Brownson, R. C. (2012). Developing the terminology for dissemination and implementation research. In R. C. Brownson, G. A. Colditz, & E. K. Proctor (Eds.), *Dissemination and implementation research in health: Translating science to practice* (pp. 23–54). New York: Oxford University Press.

Rahdert, E. H. (1991). *Adolescent Assessment Referral System manual.* Rockville, MD: National Institute on Drug Abuse.

Rassool, G. H. (2011). *Understanding addiction behaviours: Theoretical & clinical practice in health and social care.* New York: Palgrave Macmillan.

Reed, S. C., & Evans, S. M. (2009). Research design and methodology in studies of women and addiction. In K. T. Brady, S. E. Back, & S. F. Greenfield (Eds.), *Women and addiction: A comprehensive handbook* (pp. 14–31). New York: Guilford Press.

Re-Entry Policy Council. (2004). *Report of the Re-Entry Policy Council: Charting the safe and successful return of prisoners to the community.* New York: Council of State Governments. Retrieved November 15, 2013, from http://csgjustice-center.org/reentry/publications/the-report-of-the-re-entry-policy-council-ch arting-the-safe-and-successful-return-of-prisoners-to-the-community/

Reitan, R. M. (1958). Validity of the Trail Making Test as an indicator of organic brain damage. *Perceptual and Motor Skills, 8*, 271–276.

Reoux, J. P., & Oreskovich, M. R. (2006). A comparison of two versions of the Clinical Institute Withdrawal Assessment for Alcohol: The CIWA-Ar and CIWA-AD. *American Journal on Addictions, 15*(1), 85–93.

Ribisl, K. M., Walton, M. A., Mowbray, C. T., Luke, D. A., Davidson, W. S., & Bootsmiller, B. J. (1996). Minimizing participant attrition in panel studies through the use of effective retention and tracking strategies: Review and recommendations. *Evaluation and Program Planning, 19*(1), 1–25.

Richardson, M. A. (2007). The relationship between training availability and social workers' ability to treat problem drinkers. *Journal of Drug Education, 37*, 163–175.

Richardson, M. A. (2008). Social work education: The availability of alcohol-related course curriculum and social workers' ability to work with problem drinkers. *Journal of Social Work Practice, 22*, 119–128.

Ridley, T. D., & Kordinak, S. T. (1988). Reliability and validity of the Quantitative Inventory of Alcohol Disorders (QIAD) and the veracity of self-report by alcoholics. *American Journal of Drug and Alcohol Abuse, 14*(2), 263–292.

Riskind, J. H., Beck, A. T., Berchick, R. J., Brown, G., & Steer, R. A. (1987). Reliability of DSM-III diagnoses for major depression and generalized anxiety disorder using the structured clinical interview for DSM-III. *Archives of General Psychiatry, 44*(9), 817–820.

Robins, L. N., Wing, J., Wittchen, H. U., Helzer, J. E., Babor, T. F., Burke, J., et al. (1988). The Composite International Diagnostic Interview: An epidemiologic instrument suitable for use in conjunction with different diagnostic systems and in different cultures. *Archives of General Psychiatry, 45,* 1069–1077.

Robinson, W. (1950). Ecological correlations and the behavior of individuals. *American Sociological Review, 15,* 351–357.

Rogers, E. M. (1995a). Diffusion of drug abuse prevention programs: Spontaneous diffusion, agenda setting, and reinvention. In T. E. Backer, S. L. David, & G. Soucy (Eds.), *Reviewing the behavioral science knowledge base on technology transfer* (pp. 90–105). NIDA Research Monograph 155, NIH Publication No. 95-4035. Rockville, MD: National Institute on Drug Abuse.

Rogers, E. M. (1995b). *Diffusion of innovations* (5th ed.). New York: Free Press.

Rollnick, S., Heather, N., Gold, R., & Hall, W. (1992). Development of a short "readiness to change" questionnaire for use in brief, opportunistic interventions among excessive drinkers. *British Journal of Addiction, 87,* 743–754.

Roman, P. M., & Johnson, J. A. (2002). Adoption and implementation of new technologies in substance abuse treatment. *Journal of Substance Abuse Treatment, 22,* 211–218.

Rosenberg, H. (1993). Prediction of controlled drinking by alcoholics and problem drinkers. *Psychological Bulletin, 113,* 129–139.

Rounsaville, B. J., Carroll, K. M., & Onken, L. S. (2001). A stage model of behavioral therapies research: Getting started and moving on from stage I. *Clinical Psychology: Science and Practice, 8*(2), 133–142.

Royse, D., Thyer, B. A., Padgett, D. K., & Logan, T. K. (2001). *Program evaluation: An introduction* (3rd ed.). Belmont, CA: Wadsworth, Brooks/Cole.

Rubin, A., & Babie, E. R. (2005). *Research methods for social work* (5th ed.). Belmont, CA: Thomson/Brooks Cole.

Rubin, A., & Parrish, D. E. (2011). Validation of the evidence-based practice process assessment scale-short version. *Research on Social Work Practice, 21,* 200–211.

Ruiz-Primo, M. A. (2006). *A multi-method and multi-source approach for studying fidelity of implementation.* Center for the Study of Evaluation Report 677. Los Angeles: University of California Los Angeles, National Center for Research on Evaluation, Standards, and Student Testing. Retrieved from http://www.cse. ucla.edu/products/reports/R677.pdf

Rush, B. R., & Morisano, D. (2010). Going off the rails for "love or money": Implementation issues related to payment of research participants in an addiction-research project. In D. L. Streiner & S. Sidani (Eds.), *When research goes off the rails: Why it happens and what you can do about it* (pp. 43–51). New York: Guilford Press.

Russell, M. (1994). New assessment tools for drinking in pregnancy: T-ACE, TWEAK, and others. *Alcohol Health and Research World, 18*(1), 55–61.

Ryan, J. P., Marsh, J. C., Testa, M. F., & Louderman, R. (2006). Integrating substance abuse treatment and child welfare services: Findings from the Illinois alcohol and other drug abuse waiver demonstration. *Social Work Research, 30*(2), 95–107.

Saleh, S. S., Vaughn, T., Levey, S., Fuortes, L., Uden-Holmen, T., & Hall, J. A. (2006). Cost–effectiveness of case management in substance abuse treatment. *Research on Social Work Practice, 16*(1), 38–47.

Salganik, M. J., & Heckathorn, D. D. (2004). Sampling and estimation in hidden populations using respondent-driven sampling. *Sociological Methodology, 34*, 193–239.

Sanchez, R., Dunteman, G., Kuo, J., Yu, D., & Bray, R. (2001). Estimating substance abuse treatment needs using social indicators. Center for Substance Abuse Treatment.

Sayette, M. A., Shiffman, S., Tiffany, S. T., Niaura, R. S., Martin, C. S., & Shadel, W. G. (2000). Methodological approaches to craving research: The measurement of drug craving. *Addiction, 95*(Suppl. 2), S189–S210.

Schaub, M., Stevens, A., Berto, D., Hunt, N., Kerschl, V., McSweeney, T., et al. (2010). Comparing outcomes of "voluntary" and "quasi-compulsory" treatment of substance dependence in Europe. *European Addiction Research, 16*(1), 53–60.

Schori, M. (2011). Valuation of drug abuse: A review of current methodologies and implications for policy making. *Research on Social Work Practice, 21*(4), 421–431.

Schwartz, S. (1994). The fallacy of the ecological fallacy: The potential misuse of a concept and the consequences. *American Journal of Public Health, 84*(5), 819–824.

Scott, C. (2004). A replicable model for achieving over 90% follow-up rates in longitudinal studies of substance abusers. *Drug and Alcohol Dependence, 74*, 21–36.

Seddon, T. (2005). Paying drug users to take part in research: Justice, human rights and business perspectives on the use of incentive payments. *Addiction Research and Theory, 13*(2), 101–109.

Selzer, M. L. (1971). The Michigan Alcoholism Screening Test (MAST): The quest for a new diagnostic instrument. *American Journal of Psychiatry, 127*, 1653–1658.

Senreich, E., & Straussner, S. L. A. (2013). The effect of MSW education on students' knowledge and attitudes regarding substance abusing clients. *Journal of Social Work Education, 49*(2), 321–336.

Shadish, W. R., Cook, T. D., & Campbell, D. T. (2002). *Experimental and quasi-experimental designs for generalized causal inference.* New York: Houghton Mifflin/Wadsworth.

Sheehan, D. V., Lecrubier, Y., Sheehan, K. H., Amorim, P., Janavs, J., Weiller, E., et al. (1998). The Mini-International Neuropsychiatric Interview (MINI): The development and validation of a structured diagnostic psychiatric interview for DSM-IV and ICD-20. *Journal of Clinical Psychiatry, 59*(Suppl. 20), 22–33.

Sheridan, M. J. (1995). A psychometric assessment of the Children of Alcoholics Screening Test (CAST). *Journal of Studies on Alcohol, 56*, 156–160.

Shillington, A. M., & Clapp, J. D. (2000). Self-report stability of adolescent substance use: Are there differences for gender, ethnicity and age? *Drug and Alcohol Dependence, 60*, 19–27.

Sidora-Arcoleo, K., & Frick, K. (2012). Cost–effectiveness analyses for intervention studies. In B. M. Melnyk & D. Morrison-Beedy (Eds.), *Intervention research: Designing, conducting, analyzing, and funding* (pp. 331–342). New York: Springer.

Sidora-Arcoleo, K., & McClain, D. B. (2012). Explaining intervention effects. In B. M. Melynk & D. Morrison-Beedy (Eds.), *Intervention research: Designing, conducting, analyzing, and funding* (pp. 343–359). New York: Springer.

Siegel, S. (2005). Drug tolerance, drug addiction, and drug anticipation. *Current Directions in Psychological Science, 14*(6), 296–300.

Simeone, R., Frank, B., & Aryan, Z. (1993). Needs assessment in substance misuse: A comparison of approaches and a case study. *International Journal of the Addictions, 28*(8), 767–792.

Simpson, D. D. (2002). A conceptual framework for transferring research into practice. *Journal of Substance Abuse Treatment, 22*(4), 171–182.

Simpson, D. D., Joe, G. W., & Broome, K. M. (2002). A national 5–year follow-up of treatment outcomes for cocaine dependence. *Archives of General Psychiatry, 59*, 538–544.

Simpson, D. D., Joe, G. W., & Brown, B. S. (1997). Treatment retention and follow-up outcomes in the Drug Abuse Treatment Outcome Study (DATOS). *Psychology of Addictive Behaviors, 114*(4), 297–307.

Singer, J. D., & Willett, J. B. (2003). *Applied longitudinal data analysis: Modeling change and event occurrence.* New York: Oxford University Press.

Singer, M. (2009). *Introduction to syndemics: A critical systems approach to public and community health.* San Francisco: John Wiley & Sons.

Sink, C., & Mvududu, N. (2010). Statistical power, sampling, and effect sizes: Three keys to research relevancy. *Counseling Outcome Research and Evaluation, 1*(2), 1–18.

Skinner, H. A. (1982). The Drug Abuse Screening Test. *Addictive Behavior, 7*(4), 363–367.

Skloot, R. (2011). *The immortal life of Henrietta Lacks.* New York: Random House.

Smedslund, G., Berg, R. C., Hammerstrom, K. T., Steiro, A., Leiknes, K. A., Dayl, H. M., et al. (2011). Motivational interviewing is a short psychological treatment that can help people cut down on drugs and alcohol. *Cochrane Database of Systematic Reviews, 5,* CD008063.

Smith, M. J. W., Whitaker, T., & Weismiller, T. (2006). Social workers in the substance abuse treatment field: A snapshot of service activities. *Health & Social Work, 31*(2), 109–115.

Sobell, L. C., Maisto, S. A., Sobell, M. B., & Cooper, A. M. (1979). Reliability of alcohol abusers' self-reports of drinking behavior. *Behaviour Research and Therapy, 17,* 157–160.

Sobell, L. C., & Sobell, M. B. (2000). Alcohol timeline followback (TLFB). In *Handbook of psychiatric measures* (pp. 477–479). Washington, DC: American Psychiatric Association.

Sobell, L. C., Sobell, M. B., Leo, G. I., Agrawal, S., Johnson-Young, L., & Cunningham, J. A. (2002). Promoting self-change with alcohol abusers: A community-level mail intervention based on natural recovery studies. *Alcoholism: Clinical and Experimental Research, 26*(6), 936–948.

Solomon, P. L., Cavanaugh, M. M., & Draine, J. (2009). *Randomized controlled trials: Design and implementation for community-based psychosocial interventions. Pocket Guides to Social Work Research Methods.* New York: Oxford University Press.

Sorensen, J. L., Lin, C. Y., & Sera, R. E. (2004). Technology transfer in drug abuse treatment. Annotated bibliography (2nd ed.). Retrieved on October 24, 2012, from http://www.nattc.org/resPubs/ttdat_bibliography.pdf

Stanhope, V., Solomon, P., Pernell-Arnold, A., Sands, R. G., & Bourjoll, J. N. (2005). Evaluating cultural competence among behavioral health professionals. *Psychiatric Rehabilitation Journal, 28*(3), 225–233.

Steele-Johnson, D., Narayan, A., Delgado, K. M., & Cole, P. (2010). Pretraining influences and readiness to change dimensions: A focus on status versus dynamic issues. *Journal of Applied Behavioral Science, 46*(2), 245–274.

Steenrod, S. (2009). A functional guide to the evidence-based practice movement in the substance abuse treatment field. *Journal of Social Work Practice in the Addictions, 9*(4), 353–365.

Stelk, W. J. (2006). Implementing health-care innovations: In search of a theoretical foundation for a science of implementation. *International Journal of Mental Health, 35*(2), 35–49.

Stewart, S. H., Goldmann, A., Neumann, T., & Spies, C. (2010). Biomarkers of alcohol and other drug use. In P. G. Miller, J. Strang, & P. M. Miller (Eds.), *Addiction research methods* (pp. 147–162). Hoboken, NJ: Wiley-Blackwell/ Addiction Press.

Stone, A. A., Shiffman, S., Atienza, A. A., & Nebeling, L. (Eds.). (2007). *The science of real-time data capture: Self-reports in health research.* New York: Oxford University Press.

Straussner, S., Naegle, M., Gillespie, C., Wolkstein, E., Donath, R., & Azmitia, E. (2006). The SATOL Project: An interdisciplinary model of technology transfer for research-to-practice in clinical supervision for addiction treatment. *Journal of Evidence-Based Social Work, 3*(3/4), 39–54.

Straussner, S. L. A. (2001). *Ethnocultural factors in substance abuse treatment.* New York: Guilford Press.

Straussner, S. L. A. (2013). *Clinical work with substance abusing clients* (3rd ed.). New York: Guilford Press.

Straussner, S. L. A., & Vairo, E. (2007). The impact of a post-master's program in substance abuse on social work and other health professionals. *Journal of Teaching in Social Work, 27,* 105–123.

Substance Abuse and Mental Health Services Administration. (2004). *Clinical preventive services in substance abuse and mental health update: From science to services.* DHHS Publication No. (SMA) 04-3906. Rockville, MD: Department of Health and Human Services.

Center for Substance Abuse Treatment. The Role of Biomarkers in the Treatment of Alcohol Use Disorders. *Substance Abuse Treatment Advisory.* Volume 5, Issue 4, September 2006. Substance Abuse and Mental Health Services Administration. (2010). *Results from the 2009 National Survey on Drug Use and Health: Vol. 1. Summary of national findings.* NSDUH Series H-38A, HHS Publication No. SMA 10-4586. Rockville, MD: Office of Applied Studies. Retrieved February 6, 2012, from http://oas.samhsa.gov/ NSDUH/2k9NSDUH/2k9ResultsP.pdf

Substance Abuse and Mental Health Services Administration. (2012a). *Advisory: The role of biomarkers in the treatment of alcohol use disorders, 2012 revision.* HHS Publication No. (SMA) 12-4686. Retrieved November 15, 2013, from http://store.samhsa.gov/product/The-Role-of-Biomarkers-in-the-T reatment-of-Alcohol-Use-Disorders-2012-Revision/SMA12-4686

Substance Abuse and Mental Health Services Administration. (2012b). *Results from the 2011 National Survey on Drug Use and Health: Summary of national findings.* NSDUH series H-44, HHS Publication No. (SMA) 12-4713. Rockville, MD: Office of Applied Studies. Retrieved December 17, 2012, from http:// www.samhsa.gov/data/NSDUH/2k11Results/NSDUHresults2011.pdf

Sullivan, C., Rumptz, M., Campbell, R., Eby, K., & Davidson, W. (1996). Retaining participants in longitudinal community research: A comprehensive protocol. *Journal of Applied Behavioral Science, 32*(3), 262–276.

Sullivan, J. T., Sykora, K., Schneiderman, J., Naranjo, C. A., & Sellers, E. M. (1989). Assessment of alcohol withdrawal: The revised Clinical Institute Withdrawal Assessment for Alcohol scale (CIWA-Ar). *British Journal of Addiction, 84,* 1353–1357.

Sun, A. (2001). Systematic barriers to the employment of social workers in alcohol and other drug treatment agencies: A statewide survey. *Journal of Social Work Practice in the Addictions, 1*(1), 11–24.

Sun, A. P. (2009). *Helping substance-abusing women of vulnerable populations: Effective treatment principles and strategies.* New York: Columbia University Press.

Sung, N. S., Crowley, W. F., Genel, M., Salber, P., Sandy, L., Sherwood, L. M., et al. (2003). Central challenges facing the national clinical research enterprise [Electronic version]. *Journal of the American Medical Association, 289*(10), 1278–1287.

Tarter, R. E. (1990). Evaluation and treatment of adolescent substance abuse: A decision tree method. *American Journal of Drug and Alcohol Abuse, 16,* 1–46.

Tartar, R. E., & Kirisci, L. (1997). The Drug Use Screening Inventory for adults: Psychometric structure and discriminative sensitivity. *American Journal of Drug and Alcohol Abuse, 23,* 207–219.

Tashakkori, A., & Teddlie, C. (Eds.). (2003). *Handbook of mixed methods in social & behavioral research.* Thousand Oaks, CA: Sage.

Thombs, D. L., O'Mara, R. J., Tsukamoto, M., Rossheim, M. E., Weiller, R. M., Merves, M. L., et al. (2010). Event-level analyses of energy drink consumption and alcohol intoxication in bar patrons. *Addictive Behaviors, 35*(4), 325–330.

Thurstin, A. H., & Alfano, A. M. (1988). The association of alcoholic subtype with treatment outcome: An 18-month follow-up. *Substance Use & Misuse, 23*(3), 321–330.

Tiffany, S., Friedman, L., Greenfield, S., Hasin, D., & Jackson, R. (2012). Beyond drug use: A systematic consideration of other outcomes in evaluations of treatments for substance use disorders. *Addiction, 107*(4), 709–718.

Toerien, M., Brookes, S. T., Metcalfe, C., de Salis, I., Tomlin, Z., Peters, T. J., et al. (2009). A review of reporting of participant recruitment and retention in RCTs in six major journals. *Trials, 10*(1), 52–64.

Trikalinos, T. A., Salanti, G., Zintzara, E., & Ioannidis, J. P. (2008). Meta-analysis methods. *Advances in Genetics, 60,* 311–334.

Tripodi, S., Bledsoe, S., Kim, J., & Bender, K. (2011). Effects of correctional-based programs for female inmates: A systematic review. *Research on Social Work Practice, 21*(1), 15–31.

Tucker, A. R., & Blythe, B. (2009). Attention to treatment fidelity in social work outcomes: A review of the literature from the 1990s. *Social Work Research, 32*(3), 185–190.

Tucker, J. A., & Simpson, C. A. (2011). The recovery spectrum: From self-change to seeking treatment. *Alcohol Research & Health, 33*(4), 371–379.

van Saane, N., Sluiter, J., Verbeek, J., & Fings-Dresen, M. (2003). Reliability and validity of instruments measuring job satisfaction—A systematic review. *Occupational Medicine, 53*(3), 191–200.

van Wormer, K., & Davis, D. R. (2013). *Addiction treatment: A strengths perspective* (3rd ed.). Belmont, CA: Brooks Cole/Cengage Learning.

van Wormer, K., & Thyer, B. A. (2010). Preface; Introduction to evidence-based practice; and Evidence-based practice in the area of substance abuse. In K. van Wormer & B. A. Thyer (Eds.), *Evidence-based practice in the field of substance abuse: A book of readings,* (pp. vii–11). Los Angeles: Sage.

Vaughn, M. G., & Perron, B. E. (2013). *Social work practice in the addictions.* New York: Springer.

Wallace, L., & Turner, F. (2009). A systematic review of psychometric evaluation of motivational interviewing integrity measures. *Journal of Teaching in the Addictions, 8*(1/2), 84–123.

Walters, G. (2000). Spontaneous remission from alcohol, tobacco, and other drug abuse: Seeing quantitative answers to qualitative questions. *American Journal of Drug and Alcohol Abuse, 26*(3), 443–460.

Walton, M., Ramanathan, C., & Reischl, T. (1998). Tracking substance abusers in longitudinal research: Understanding follow-up contact difficulty. *American Journal of Community Psychology, 26*(2), 233–253.

Wandersman, A., Duffy, J., Flaspohler, P., Noonan, R., Lubell, K., Stillman, L., et al. (2008). Bridging the gap between prevention research and practice: The interactive systems framework for dissemination and implementation. *American Journal of Community Psychology, 41*, 171–181.

Warren, K. R., Hewitt, B. G., & Thomas, J. D. (2011). Fetal alcohol spectrum disorders: Research challenges and opportunities. *Alcohol Research & Health, 34*(1), 4–14.

Weiner, B. J., Amick, H., & Lee, S. Y. D. (2008). Conceptualization and measurement of organizational readiness for change: A review of the literature in health services research and other fields. *Medical Care Research and Review, 65*, 379–436.

Wells, K., & Littell, J. H. (2009). Study quality assessment in systematic review of research on intervention effects. *Research on Social Work Practice, 19*(1), 52–62.

Wells, R., Lemak, C. H., & D'Aunno, T. (2005). Organizational survival in the outpatient treatment sector 1988–2000. *Medical Care Research and Review, 62*, 697–719.

Wendler, D., & Grady, C. (n.d.). *Ethical issues in research with special populations*. National Institutes of Health Clinical Center, Department of Bioethics. Retrieved November 15, 2013, from http://www.bioethics.nih.gov/research/pdf/special-populations.pdf

Westfall, J. M., Mold, J., & Fagnan, L. (2007). Practice-based research—"Blue Highways" on the NIH roadmap. *Journal of the American Medical Association, 297*(4), 403–406.

WHO ASSIST Working Group (2002). The Alcohol, Smoking and Substance Involvement Screening Test (ASSIST): Development, reliability and feasibility. *Addiction, 97,* 1183–1194.

Williams, J. S. (2003). Cognitive deficits in marijuana smokers persist after use stops. *NIDA Notes, 18*(5). Retrieved March 6, 2012, from http://archives.drugabuse.gov/NIDA_Notes/NNVol18N5/Cognitive.html

Wilson, S., Cunningham-Burley, S., Bancroft, A., Backett-Milburn, K., & Masters, H. (2007). Young people, biographical narratives and the life grid: Young people's accounts of parental substance use. *Qualitative Research, 7*(1), 135–151.

World Health Organization. (2010). Report on the meeting on indicators for monitoring alcohol, drugs and other psychoactive substance use, substance-attributable harm and societal responses, Valencia, Spain 19–21 October 2009. Retrieved September 13, 2012, from http://whqlibdoc.who.int/publications/2010/9789241500883_eng.pdf

Zarkin, G., Dunlap, L., Bray, J., & Wechsberg, W. (2002). The effect of treatment completion and length of stay on employment and crime in outpatient drug-free treatment. *Journal of Substance Abuse Treatment, 23*(2), 261–271.

Zarkin, G. A., Bray, J. W., Aldridge, A., Mitra, D., Mills, M. J., Couper, D. J., et al. (2008). Cost and cost–effectiveness of the COMBINE Study in alcohol-dependent patients. *Archives of General Psychiatry, 65*(1), 1214–1221.

Zivich, J. M. (1981). Alcoholic subtypes and treatment effectiveness. *Journal of Consulting and Clinical Psychology, 49*(1), 72–80.

Zweben, A., Barrett, D., Berger, L., & Tobin Murray, K. (2005). Recruiting and retaining participates in a combined behavioral and pharmacological clinical trial. *Journal of Studies on Alcohol, 66*(4), 72–81.

Zweben, A., Pettinati, H. M., Weiss, R. D., Youngblood, M., Cox, C. E., Mattson, M. E., et al. (2008). Relationship between medication adherence and treatment outcomes: The COMBINE study. *Alcoholism: Clinical and Experimental Research, 32*(9), 1661–1669.

Index